To Virginia,

Bryan Davis

Psalm 78:1-8

# the Image of a Father

## of a

### Father

*Reflections of God
for today's father*

# BRYAN DAVIS

# the
# Image
## of a
# Father

*Reflections of God
for today's father*

Advancing the Ministries of the Gospel

**AMG** *Publishers*

*God's Word to you is our highest calling.*

*To my darling wife, Susie,*
*without whom I would never be a father.*
*Without your love, I would never want to be.*

# Contents

# Foreword

In the late 1980s, some church educators objected to calling God a father. They insisted that their denomination delete all such references from Sunday school material. (I'm delighted to say they didn't succeed.) They pointed to the children who had grown up with abusive or neglectful parents. They also cited minorities who rarely had a permanent male figure in their lives.

"They hate the word *father* because they've never experienced a warm, caring relationship from their male parent. They've only seen the worst side of males. How can they relate?" one educator said to me.

"They relate because they know what they don't have," I argued. "They may not know what it feels like to be loved by a human father, but they certainly have some sense of what they're missing. Doesn't that make the concept of the fatherhood of God even more important?"

We continued to debate, but the last thing I said was, "If we don't emphasize that God loves us as the Perfect Father, we have not properly represented God."

The woman educator never agreed with me, but I believe I was correct. Part of my insistence was because of my own experience. Unlike Bryan Davis's children, I didn't grow up in a loving environment. Dad never hugged me or ever said he loved me. In fact, I never heard Dad ever use the word *love*.

That deficit in my life never turned me away from reciting the Lord's Prayer by saying, "Our Father who art in heaven . . ." As I said those words, I yearned to experience a love I had not known.

In fact, one event stands out clearly in my mind. I became a believer in my early twenties. On one of the first Sundays after my conversion, I heard a sermon that emphasized the fatherhood of God. For more than half an hour, the minister tried to make the connection that a good human parent's responsibility is to reflect the perfection of the heavenly. He explained that God had chosen that word to show the most loving relationship to humanity. He also pointed out the wide disparity between human roles and the perfect Fatherhood. He wanted us males—especially those with children—to realize that our responsibility was to reflect the character of the One who enabled us to be born anew in the heavenly family.

That's what Bryan Davis tries to do with this book. He isn't perfect and (to my relief) he doesn't try to come across that way. He does come across as a human and sometimes fallible father who loves his children and strives to project a true image of fatherhood that points to the Perfect One.

The author repeatedly reminds us that we have the opportunity to provide the nurturing environment that will eventually make our children yearn to honor and love the heavenly Parent. If we strive to provide the best nurturing relationship, we will have done the best we can for our children.

No one except Jesus is the perfect reflection of God, but this book points fathers in the right direction—reflecting the perfect image of the heavenly Father.

Cecil Murphey[*]

---

[*]Cecil ("Cec") Murphey has written, cowritten, or ghostwritten eighty-nine books including the million-copy seller, *Gifted Hands: the Ben Carson Story*. His latest books include *The God Who Pursues* and *The Relentless God*.

# Acknowledgments

To my heavenly Father, the perfect image of a father, thank you for loving me and showing me the Way. As a father, I am still a little child stepping into Your enormous shoes, hoping to imitate Your ways and walk in Your steps.

To my earthly father, who instilled in me a host of values I still hold precious, thank you for teaching me the importance of hard work and perseverance.

To my writing friends, thank you for helping me persevere, especially Rosemary Upton, Kistler London, Elaine Colvin, Jean Dickman, Donna Tinsley, Billie Wilson, Tom Tacker, and Cecil Murphey, encouragers who have been at my side for many years.

To everyone at AMG Publishers, especially my editor, Dan Penwell, and to my agent, Steve Laube, thank you for believing in me.

Bryan Davis is both an accomplished writer and speaker. To contact him about speaking at your church or group, or just to send him a note, you can e-mail Bryan at: bryan@imageofafather.com or visit him at his website: http://www.imageofafather.com.

# Introduction

With summer twilight casting a feather-soft glow on my daughter's drooping eyes, I sing her toward dreamland, each word shushed in an envelope of whispers.

> O Lord, You're beautiful.
> Your face is all I seek.
> For when Your eyes are on this child,
> Your grace abounds to me.[1]

I kiss her forehead and watch her gentle smile fade. Tight wrinkles dig into her brow, signaling a question at the crossroads of her mind. "Daddy?" she asks, her eyes fluttering open. "What does God look like?"

---

[1] Lyrics by Keith Green. © Birdwing Music/BMG Songs. All rights reserved. Used by permission.

What a question! How can I possibly answer it? A hundred duties await my attention. Every night brings a tug-of-war of fatherly responsibilities. On one side, the busy work of bills and fix-it projects pull like gargantuan gods, but they must wait for every juvenile head to finally nestle in its pillow. On the other side, the peaceful solitude of gentle lullabies and butterfly kisses pull back, nightly reveries with my children that transcend time. Tonight my daughter wins the battle and I tuck her covers in at the sides as I try to think of an answer that will make sense to her world of concrete realities.

"Jesus told us that God is spirit," I begin. "We can't see our heavenly Father with our eyes, but we can sort of see Him by watching other people."

"Like who?"

"Well, that's an easy one. Remember what Jesus said? 'He who has seen Me has seen the Father.' Jesus is full of truth, mercy, and love. So is God the Father. If we watch Jesus, we'll know what God the Father is like."

"But Jesus isn't here anymore. I can't watch Him."

I stroke her hair, aware of her lovely lack of abstract thought. She's right. Jesus isn't here anymore. Though I could explain the theological truth of "Christ in us," the indwelling Holy Spirit who reveals the character of God to our hearts and minds, such a nebulous concept is surely out of her reach. There no longer walks a flesh and blood Savior who fills our eyes with the Father's glory. At this moment I fully realize the gravity of my position in her sight, and its burden squeezes my chest. Dare I tell her my thoughts?

I take a deep breath and draw my hands back to my lap. "Then it's up to me to show you what God looks like."

She grins at me, her sleepiness chased away by playful thoughts. "Really? Did you go up to heaven and take a picture of Him or something?"

I poke her nose with my finger. "No, silly goose. It's just that I'm your father, and it's my job to show you what God is like. When God makes a father, He pours a bunch of His own qualities into him, the stuff that makes good fathers."

"Like what?"

"Like protection, guidance, and—" I pause for effect and then tickle her ribs. "And anything that makes you smile."

She giggles and pushes my arms away, and I gently take her hands into mine. When she settles down, she grins again and says, "I think I'd rather have a picture."

I straighten my frame, my head held high, absurdly showing off my profile. "Well, then, think of me as your picture of God." We both laugh, and I tuck her in tightly once more, whispering to settle her thoughts. "I can't be everything God is, sweetheart, but I can show you how He loves you like a father. I'm not a picture from a camera, but I am like an image of His fathering ways." I caress her cheek with tender fingers and add, "Will that be enough?"

She smiles and her eyes begin drooping again, her voice stretching into a yawn. "That'll be enough."

I watch her eyelids close, and I sigh. Will I be able to fulfill my promise? Can I possibly bridge the gap between heaven and earth and reflect God's perfect love in a way she can understand?

What does God look like, anyway? Do I know Him well enough myself? I pray that my feeble attempts will be empowered by God's own desire to show His fathering character to my children.

With tears welling in my eyes, I finish my song, hoping my sweet girl will learn the everlasting song of God's love, fusing her soul with God as she bears witness of His fathering heart in mine.

> I want to take Your word and shine it all around;
> But first, help me just to live it, Lord.
> And when I'm doing well
> Help me to never seek a crown;
> For my reward is giving glory to You.

# The Father as Life-giver

## ✧ Emotional Attachment

> He will exult over you with joy,
> He will be quiet in His love,
> He will rejoice over you with shouts of joy. (Zeph. 3:17)

I'll never forget our baby's first cry; it came right after mine. Well, it wasn't really my first cry, but it was the first emotional, out-of-control, let-it-all-hang-out cry of joy I can remember expressing. After I coached my wonderful wife, Susie, through the ordeal of labor, the sight of a little human being proceeding from the body of

my God-given helpmate brought an avalanche of feelings. The surprise of discovery and the ecstasy of sheer joy sucked the breath
right out of my lungs, and with an overwhelming sense of relief, my
breath came roaring back in shivering anthems of praise and thanksgiving. I grasped Susie's hand in both of mine and just stared at that
tiny human, complete with moving parts and covered with a pasty
white film. He seemed foreign somehow, yet familiar. After all those
months, the one we had waited for was here; our baby had arrived.
It didn't matter that his little face contorted on his cone-shaped
head. This was my son, my firstborn.

With a whoop and a holler I let the world know, "Praise the
Lord! O thank you, God!" and my little son chimed in, echoing not
only deep, primal emotions but also gratitude that the traumatic
journey was finally over. His squeaky cry was sweet music, his oval,
toothless mouth opening and closing in wailing wonder at the lights,
the people, and the strange noises. Soon, he was quiet, his wide, vio-
let eyes searching for the source of the sound, the familiar murmur-
ing he had heard while yet in the womb. He heard our voices. Our
voices, once shrouded by barriers of flesh, now blared distinct
and clear, a comforting reminder that not all was new. The loving
embrace of his uterine home gave way to an embrace more tactile
and firm, yet with the same old voices that sang him to sleep in the
darkness of the womb.

Fathers, while we may think this is the beginning of fatherhood,
our intimate relationship with our children has its genesis before we
can even see those newborn eyes wincing in their bright new world.
For our part, we are the expectant fathers, reflecting the same kind
of excitement God our Father expresses for those He created in His
image. We see the Father's joy throughout the Scriptures:

And He brought forth His people with joy,
His chosen ones with a joyful shout. (Ps. 105:43)

God our Father is the life-giver, somehow implanting Himself in each human being. He imparts the breath of life, animating this flesh-bearing image of Himself.

> Then the Lord God formed man of dust from the ground, and breathed into his nostrils the breath of life; and man became a living being. (Gen. 2:7)

All through the Bible we see a loving Father taking people by the hand, guiding them through life, blessing them with rewards and discipline, rejoicing over their triumphs when they follow His commands, and expressing sorrow over their disobedience. Each person is more than just another creature on this divine experiment called Earth. Human beings are a manifestation of God's image in His created order.

In the same way, fathers, our children are images of us. They are our offspring, springing from our bodies through the vessels of our wives. In one sense, like God, we are life-givers. Although the power to create life always comes from God, He has given us the authority and responsibility to use our bodies to create life, and the seeds we plant establish that new life as impressions of ourselves.

God rejoices over His children and cherishes them. We should do the same, demonstrating our love to our sons and daughters by expressing that love outwardly. Such a display of emotional transparency is difficult for some men; they don't come by it naturally. Many have been taught that men aren't supposed to let their emotions show, that doing so is a sign of weakness or lack of control. I've hesitated at times, wondering if I should shed a tear or laugh out loud. When I consciously think, however, about God my Father shouting with joy over me, it helps me share my emotional joy with my children. I can break out with a laughing roar and round up my little ones in big bear hugs. The freedom to fearlessly emote is truly liberating.

Our responsibility to show love to our children begins before they're born. Again, God is our model.

> For Thou didst form my inward parts;
> Thou didst weave me in my mother's womb. (Ps. 139:13)

> Before I formed you in the womb I knew you,
> And before you were born I consecrated you. (Jer. 1:5)

For a while, fathers, it will seem there is little you can do to express your love for the baby in the womb. The growth in your wife's abdomen takes no human shape on the outside; it's just a big lump. Even when glimpsed on the sonogram at the doctor's office, it doesn't always appear to be human, just an ambiguous blob that sort of looks like it might be a baby if you squint at it just right.

We might be tempted just to hang back and let our wives take care of everything in this nine-month odyssey. When the baby comes out, then we'll do our thing. It's true that Mom is the focus during pregnancy; she's giving her body to this miracle called gestation. The baby gains all its nourishment directly from her, lending to the popular notion that the burden is Mom's to bear.

Men, try to imagine carrying an anvil in your belly, and not just an ordinary anvil, but one with hands that grab your intestines, tying them into a tight sailor's knot. This anvil bounces on a trampoline and does flips and cartwheels every time you try to sleep. It gets worse. It pours toxic waste onto your stomach lining, making you feel deathly sick, and while you suffer with a digestive system that only works backward, people are telling you how happy you must be to be carrying around your darling little bundle. Such is the burden your wife carries. Don't you dare let her carry it alone. More on that in a moment.

As our children grow, their emotional nurturing process continues. A father demonstrates God's love to his growing offspring by showing a caring and compassionate heart. The simple act of taking a son on your lap and reading a book or reaching for your daughter's hand when walking through the store tells that child "I love you" more powerfully than your words ever could. Children need time with you and much more; they need your heart-to-heart communication. When a child asks you to "come and see," he needs to see real smiles and authentic excitement over his accomplishments, not, "Hey, that's great—Honey, where's the TV schedule?"

When one of my children says "Come and see," I try to make a specific remark about the new object of excitement. When my son Caleb showed me his latest Lego creation, I commented on the color scheme and asked him how the moving parts worked. Even if I'm not particularly interested, forcing myself to take notice induces authentic interest. As my son answered the questions, I felt the emotional part of love and caring well up inside. *This boy is really a neat guy! He's thought this project through, and I love how his mind works!*

And boys differ from girls in the way they receive our interaction. My sons enjoy more seismic, athletic pursuits than do my daughters. They delight in roughhousing on the family room floor, baseball in the yard, and tennis anywhere we can find a court. Even though our masculinity dominates, I try to ensure that I reach their tender side as well. A quick pat on the back, a gentle word of appreciation or sorrow, a firm hug of celebration or sympathy can work wonders in a young man's psyche.

When Caleb had an infected hip joint, I stayed with him after surgery, reading to him, making up stories, and taking care of his physical needs for two days and nights. Our time together involved physical contact, turning him for comfort, helping him dress, and taking care of other bodily needs. The experience created emotional bonds that have lasted ever since, but with boys, these times are personal. We nurture them privately, man-to-man, not in the public arena.

Boys typically don't want to hold hands in public. The act communicates a need for support or protection. Boys want their fathers to be with them in partnership, two soldiers in a foxhole. "I'll cover you and you'll cover me." Of course when the going gets tough, they're glad for your leadership and protective strength, but it's important for you to display your admiration of their masculinity. Be a partner. Slap him on the back and give him a high five. Buy him a slice of pizza after the game, win or lose. Teach him the sanctity of the old fishing hole, the fine art of arm wrestling, and the pleasure of an open-field football tackle. Show him how to be strong, openly display your passion for protecting your family, and, above all, let him see how much you love your wife. In other words, show him biblical manliness, the masculine side of God our Father.

There will come a time when you should give your son a strong, sympathetic hug, and you'll know when that time comes. A crisis will be tearing his soul apart, and the signs will be clear. He'll be crying. Never, ever say big boys don't cry. They do. And when he does, he needs his foxhole partner to pick him up. It's time for you to cover him; he's been wounded on the field of battle.

My oldest son, James, is a six-foot-five karate enthusiast, and even though his large frame indicates strength and commands fear, he has cried in my presence on more than one occasion. He trusted me to keep his emotional turmoil between us. Yes, I am exposing it here, but the details will forever be between us and God. During those times, I held his hand and rubbed his back. Such was our camaraderie, one soldier for God pulling a wounded comrade from the battlefield and nursing his wounds. There's nothing more natural.

I've also experienced the blessing of seeing my sons care for me. On a beautiful day in autumn, we were playing an all-out, frenzied, family football game. On one play, as I ran the ball to the right, my second-born son, Josiah, stood in my way. He's hyper fast, quick and agile as a young buck, and always determined to catch dear ol' Dad. I had to turn on the jets to get past him, straining my forty something legs like an aging halfback reaching for past glories. Two hard steps and "pop!" A sound like a rifle shot snapped in my ears, and ripping pain threw me to the ground. I grasped my calf, knowing that my exuberance had stretched the muscle beyond its limits. For a few seconds I writhed in intense pain, but I'll never forget the exhilarating feeling when my two oldest boys, James and Josiah, lifted me bodily and practically carried me into the house. Their father was wounded, and it was their turn to carry me. I remember thinking, *Thank you, God. Your life-giving touch has come full circle.*

Although my daughters also like some rough-and-tumble, they usually appreciate the softer touch more than the guys do. For them, shoulder rides are better than wrestling, and holding hands in public says to the world, "Look, everyone! This is my Daddy!" Dad, you are not your daughter's partner in protection; you *are* her protector. Never invite her into the foxhole; it's not her place. Teach her to support your protective efforts and those of her brothers. Your emotional attachment with her is fulfilled as she becomes a strong and confident woman, because she has you as her protector and defender.

When I worked away from home, I occasionally received a card in the mail, a note to encourage me and lighten my day. It was always from my daughter, Arianna. She appreciated that I was laboring for her, creating a home that would give her decent shelter, and providing for her education. She wanted to help me and support me. I'm sure my coworkers could see an extra bounce in my step and a new sparkle in my eyes. My wife, Susie, and our daughters are heaven-sent gifts of life to me, and our emotional attachment is ever growing stronger, a mutual stimulus to fulfill the roles God has given us.

Fathers, if you don't display an emotional attachment with your children, you will be painting a false picture of their heavenly Father. Tragically, some view God as the great clockmaker who wound up this cosmic clock called the universe and is now just letting it tick. Such a god is not intimately involved with the details of the passing seconds. People who think this way can't pray, because, to them, God doesn't really care. They can't worship, because God isn't around to receive it. They can't be saved, because God is powerless and has left no one in charge of the cosmos. I wonder if they had fathers who gave them life and then abandoned them emotionally, skewing their perception. While surviving because of physical provision, they haven't thrived, being emotionally starved by men who could not or would not rejoice over them with shouts of joy.

## ✦ Caring for the Holy Vessel

> Then God said, "Behold, I have given you every plant yielding seed that is on the surface of all the earth, and every tree which has fruit yielding seed; it shall be food for you; and to every beast of the earth and to every bird of the sky and to every thing that moves on the earth which has life, I have given every green plant for food"; and it was so. (Gen. 1:29, 30)

As a life-giver, you're in charge of making sure the vessel that carries your child is well cared for. Your wife is that holy vessel. Even though she may suffer in godly silence, nine months of discomfort deserves to be rewarded lavishly. Don't wait for her to ask. Watch for the signs.

One of my favorite TV commercials shows a disheveled man desperately shopping in an all-night convenience store. He pulls a bag of chips from the shelf and hurries to the front window to display it for someone outside. He gets the person's approval and then proceeds to do the same for several other food products. He's tired, but you can tell that finding just the right items is his passion. Near the end of the commercial you can see that the person outside is his very pregnant wife, obviously suffering through the food cravings so common for women in her condition. The commercial is funny and perhaps stretches reality, but it conveys an important element of truth that can't be denied. The role of the father and husband is to nurture his unborn child while loving and caring for the treasured vessel that bears the burden of pregnancy.

Men, you have never felt, and you will never feel the discomfort of bearing a child. Of course I'm not the right gender to write about it experientially, but I'll give you my observations, having watched my wife go through the ordeal seven times. It seems to me the worst part of the burden is that it continues for so long. There are many pains and tribulations we can endure if we can perceive an end to the suffering, but this one seems to have no end. Yes, the due date is marked on the calendar, but she knows, as that day approaches, the burden will only get heavier. The light at the end of the tunnel is at the top of a steep, torturous incline. Every day the kicks get harder, a left to the bladder, a right to the kidneys, and a flip of the body that seems to twist her intestines into a knot. She feels like she'll never have a good night's sleep again, and a visit to the bathroom means either a time to throw up or the fifth time to urinate in the same night, but never, ever to have a normal bowel movement.

She feels huge, undesirable, and awkward. Her emotions fly from joy to anger to sadness as her hormones do a tango in her brain. The smell of your favorite food makes her sick, so you can't cook the bratwurst and onions. You walk a tightrope when it comes to intimacy. On the one hand, you embrace, cuddle, and caress her, letting her know you still find her beautiful and desirable, even though she feels like a whale in a goldfish bowl. Although you show affection, you truncate your advances, since the thought of further intimacy makes her feel even sicker than does the smell of your bratwurst.

I'll never forget the time Susie was extremely constipated during her first pregnancy. In her agonizing discomfort she asked me to run out and get an enema. Now, please understand—I was naïve, sheltered as a youth, and married young; I didn't know what an enema looked like. I had heard of them, but I had never seen one in action or in the store. After she tried to explain it to me, I went out to the local drugstore with a picture in my head. In my rush and confusion, when I tried to explain what I needed to the clerk, I'm sure I mentally pummeled out every ounce of sense he had in his head. I came home with a hot water bottle and a tube, not the nifty plastic Fleets bottle Susie had expected. My bottle looked like it might work ... maybe ... somehow, but I knew I didn't want to watch. Susie, even in her anguish, accepted it and tried to use it, having no choice at that point, such was her desperation. I don't remember the rest of the story. She's still alive and functioning, so it must have had a happy ending. What I remember is my overwhelmingly urgent desire to help my wife, to bring comfort to her tortured body. She was a willing servant, bearing my child, suffering intense pain. I knew I would shake heaven and earth to try to get what she needed. Yes, I failed that time, but at the end of the day, she knew how much I cared.

Men, show your wives how much you care. Once a woman is pregnant, the role she's filling cannot be avoided without committing the great sin of abortion. So, to obey the God she loves, she bears this burden for Him and for you willingly. Help her without complaining. Run out and buy the pickles at two in the morning, cook special meals for her, tell her how beautiful she is, and caress her loving face and tenderly hold her hand, not expecting fulfillment of your own desires. You're in this together.

## ✧ Preparation of the Home

And God saw that it was good. (Gen. 1:25)

In the days preceding the creation of man, God set up the cosmos in such a way that man could live in it comfortably. Being the life-giver, He fulfilled His responsibility to create a proper habitat for life. In the same way, we fathers are called to make a home fit for our offspring. That doesn't mean we have to build a new addition for the nursery or plaster the guestroom with bunny-covered wallpaper. We do, however, have to create a living environment that will allow a child to thrive. Although luxuries can be helpful, children don't need a big house, their own rooms, or brand-new cribs. A baby will get along just fine sleeping in your bedroom in a used bassinet snuggling a hand-me-down blanket. A father is responsible for creating a physical environment that can be deemed "good," providing nutritious food, reasonable shelter, and clothing fit for the seasons. We're to work hard to provide, not being ashamed of having less than the best but being terribly ashamed if we cannot provide the essentials of life.

Of course there are exceptions in the most destitute of times, but a dedicated father never gives up. His God-given passion is to provide for his family by doing whatever ethical work he can to gain the essentials for his home, remembering the testimony of David, "I have been young, and now I am old; yet I have not seen the righteous forsaken, or his descendants begging bread" (Ps. 37:25).

On the one month "anniversary" of our wedding day, I was fired from my first job. Fresh out of college and with no experience in the world of office politics, I didn't see the signs of a power struggle in the company, and I was pushed aside. To make matters worse, I had to take the bus that day and walk about a mile in the rain to get home from the bus stop. Although I suffered the pain and embarrassment of failure, even on that dark day I saw the light of God's love. I was believing and not despairing. I bought a single rose on the way home and presented it to my darling wife. I kissed her and wished her a happy anniversary, giving her the bad news in a matter-of-fact way. Her godly support and faith in me was a beacon in the night. We knew God would provide, and He did, as I started my new job on the day my severance pay ran out.

During that time of searching, I felt a passion for providing for Susie, and she appreciated my longing to meet her needs. As we added children to our home, my desire to supply my family's needs increased accordingly. This passion drives us to be like Him, giving sustenance to the lives we bring into the world. The role of a father in providing for his home will be covered more thoroughly in chapter 2, but for now we must all realize that being a life-giver necessitates creating a physical environment in which life can thrive.

A father also establishes in his home a healthy spiritual environment, one in which a child will understand that loving and obeying God are part of life, not an add-on exercise. Before your baby is born, make it a habit to pray with your wife. Schedule a convenient time and stick to it. Although your gestating infant won't understand your words while listening inside the womb, when he arrives, the praying environment will be in place, and your supplications will not sound strange. A house of prayer will seem natural; the daily devotional will be an expected part of each day, not a foreign concept that makes your children wonder what's wrong when you finally decide to get the family together and read the Bible. They should never find it uncomfortable or unusual to be on their knees.

In our home, we have devotions with our children each morning and evening. On occasion, we'll miss one of our meetings due to an extra busy schedule, but the omissions are rare enough that the children find the exceptions to be curious. I remember getting home very late one night after visiting friends. As I laid my sleepy daughter, Hannah, on her bed, she murmured, "Aren't we going to read the Bible tonight?" She didn't wait for an answer, falling sound asleep when her head nestled into the pillow. Her words were beautiful music to my ears, because it meant that her mind had been trained for devotion. She was so accustomed to hearing God's Word before laying her head down to sleep that the lack of its comforting presence seemed strange, like sleeping alone in the woods on a cold night.

Fathers, life-givers, never underestimate the power of the environment you create for your offspring. Even if your abode is humble and crude, your passion for provision will come through as you work hard to supply your children's true needs. Even more important, your priorities for life will be manifest as your children live in the spiritual environment you create. If devotion to God is your paramount concern, the time you spend nurturing that relationship in concert with your family will prove your intent.

## ✧ Establishing Authority

> And God blessed them; and God said to them, "Be fruitful and multiply, and fill the earth, and subdue it; and rule over the fish of the sea and over the birds of the sky, and over every living thing that moves on the earth." (Gen. 1:28)

As soon as God created man, He handed out orders. As a life-giver, our heavenly Father gave us a reason to live (see Gen. 1:28). In like manner, we fathers establish the principles of authority and obedience by making clear what we expect of our children, giving them a reason to live and giving them order so they won't wander in the world, self-deluded by a feeling of autonomy.

Even while a child is in the womb, a father can make his presence known to that child. Although a pre-born infant may not understand Dad's words, the soothing, authoritative voice of a masculine parent prepares a child to listen, recognizing that voice as soon as she is expelled into the colder, brighter world. Her father's role is not yet clear in her mind, but this beginning sets the process in motion of showing the child God the Father, the One who is intimately involved with giving life to a newborn soul and nurturing it to maturity.

As a child grows, she sees her father in charge of the home, lovingly exercising his authority, delegating it when necessary, while her mother responds faithfully to her husband's role. It's important that your children see this interchange so they can experience the wonder of willing submission on the part of your wife in response to your loving authority. This teaches them by example the position you've been given.

This development, this understanding of authority in her father's home, is crucial in her spiritual growth. The only way a child will learn that she's compelled to obey is if she's trained through a channel of authority. In other words, when we give a child a task, no matter how small, we need to reward or discipline according to how the child obeys. Even a word of praise for a job well done or a word of reproof for disregarding a command can go a long way toward enforcing the idea that you're in charge, and it presents a picture of God as One who expects obedience as well.

A father demonstrates the ultimate authority of God by establishing himself as supreme, benevolent ruler in his home. The details regarding how he properly disciplines his children could fill an entire book, and, indeed, there are many books on the subject. There are two major axioms, however, on which all discipline succeeds or fails. In order to signify authority and command respect, a father must be impartial and just, and a father must be obedient to his own authority, God.

If a father is unjust, he destroys his child's faith in him. If he punishes a child without knowing her guilt for certain, he risks injuring his authority in the child's eyes for perhaps the rest of her life. In a similar way, when a child goes unpunished while knowing her guilt, that child can lose respect for her father's authority, especially if she knows her father is also aware of her guilt.

Since we can't judge perfectly, not being omniscient, what are we to do? The bottom line is this: strive for justice with a pure heart. Don't ignore the guilt you know exists, even if your choice of discipline is only verbal admonishment, and don't punish if you're unsure of guilt. Even with these guidelines, you may make a mistake. You may find new information that proves your initial judgment wrong. In those cases, an admission of error and a heartfelt apology to your child will help heal the wounds in those found guilty unjustly, and you will gain respect in the case of one improperly exonerated.

Because of the complexity of this subject, I will cover it in greater detail in chapter 6, "The Father as Judge."

The second axiom carries even greater weight. If a father is disobedient to God, he does more damage to his authority than injustice ever could. Why should a child obey her father, the guy who sets the rules, if her father can't even obey the rules himself? The common excuse is, "Well, I'm just a sinner, so I'm going to sin once in a while." This attitude results from the notion that God, for some strange reason, has not given His followers enough grace and power to overcome sin, that Satan is an enemy we cannot consistently conquer. The Bible says the opposite:

> But in all these things we overwhelmingly conquer through Him who loved us. (Rom. 8:37)

> We know that no one who is born of God sins; but He who was born of God keeps him and the evil one does not touch him. (1 John 5:18)

Your authority figure is God. Your children must see you submitting to your Master if you expect them to submit to you. If you try to serve two masters, sometimes obeying and sometimes rebelling, you demonstrate that you have only one master, yourself. Your children will follow in your footsteps, obeying you when it's convenient and following their own way when it suits them. And why not? They're just sinners, right? Your answer should be, "May it never be! How shall we who died to sin still live in it?" (Rom. 6:2).

This axiom stands as the bottom line for fathers—obedience to God. With the power God has bestowed, you and your wife have created a life. It's up to you to provide the environment—not only the essentials of life but also whatever it takes to help that new life thrive and find the ultimate life-giver, God the heavenly Father.

## ✧ Summary

As a life-giver, a father must fulfill several responsibilities. He establishes an emotional attachment with his children through outward expressions of joy, physical nurturing, and emotional support. He cares for his wife, his God-given helpmate who sacrificially bears the burden of gestating and birthing their child. He strives to bring her physical and emotional comfort, showing his compassion and appreciation for her unselfish endurance. He prepares a home, a fit place for his offspring to dwell, providing for them physically and spiritually. He works hard to supply food, clothing, and shelter, and he sees to the spiritual stability of the home, making devotional time as natural as mealtime, demonstrating that our spiritual bread is at least as important as our physical bread. Finally, a father establishes the lines of authority, making just decisions and walking in obedience to God. Those to whom he has given life are thereby given a reason to live and are not left wandering without guidance in the world.

# The Father as Provider

## ✧ What Is a Breadwinner?

Men, I'm sure you've heard that you're breadwinners. This is, indeed, a strange term. It sounds like you're in a race, maybe a marathon, and after miles and miles of toil and sweat, you cross the finish line, your arms raised in triumph. Then, instead of your getting a trophy or one of those huge cardboard checks the size of a St. Bernard, some guy in a business suit shakes your hand and gives you a loaf of pumpernickel to take home to your family. Or maybe it means you're in a fight, a bloody struggle in a dark alley, over a loaf of Wonder Bread. After knocking your opponent silly, you snatch the bread and dash home, hoping the other guy doesn't come to his senses in time to chase you.

For some men, their breadwinning responsibilities aren't far removed from the rigors of a marathon or the fierce confrontation represented by a street fight. In some lines of work, every day is a struggle, even a life-or-death commitment. The duties of the job itself can tax a man to his limits, both physically and mentally. A policeman risks his life every time he pins on his badge. A construction worker lifts, hammers, and digs his body into exhaustion. A doctor has lives placed in his care and makes decisions that could cost someone a healthy future should he make a mistake. An office worker endures the politics of unscrupulous peers and the unreasonable demands of uncaring supervisors, and he may be called upon to bend his ethics or else lose a promotion or even his job.

And for what? On payday he has a higher balance in his bank account than the day before. After taxes, mortgage payments, the power bill, and telephone charges, he can go out and buy that loaf of bread and place it on the table for his hungry children. Such is the toil of the modern breadwinner, the traditional duty of each and every father in our land.

This is indeed a high calling, an essential duty, for the man who shirks his responsibility and forces his wife and little ones to fend for themselves proves himself a scoundrel. As the Bible says, "But if anyone does not provide for his own, and especially for those of his household, he has denied the faith, and is worse than an unbeliever" (1 Tim. 5:8).

Some men have trouble dealing with the gravity of the task. Perhaps one lacks a set of skills that an employer seeks, another doesn't have the necessary confidence to guard an employer's interests, and a third is simply lazy or self-centered, seeking an easy course in life.

Excuses aside, if employment is available, whether in self-employment or in a job from an outside source, a father or any married man has the absolute command from God to see to his family's provision. There is no excuse for sitting apathetically at home while your wife wins the bread. There is no excuse for collecting a government check while you watch television or play video games. If you lack skills, training is available from myriad sources, both public and private. Confidence is a matter of faith that can be gained by studying God's Word and learning that God is the true provider (more on that in a moment). And laziness or self-centeredness is a matter of sin, which requires repentance and turning to God.

Unlike the examples cited, most men take their breadwinning responsibility seriously, tirelessly toiling, even taking on two or three jobs to keep the pantry stocked. Even those who abandon their duties often suffer the pain of guilt, being eaten away by an inner gnawing, the unfulfilled providing heart of a man. This burden is God-given; it is a natural characteristic in the heart of a father made in the image of the heavenly Father. As Jesus told us, God the Father provides for our needs. "Look at the birds of the air, that they do not sow, neither do they reap, nor gather into barns, and yet your heavenly Father feeds them" (Matt. 6:26). It's normal, therefore, to feel the urge to do the same for our "birds of the air," the little ones God puts in our nest.

The framework of this verse, however, provides a broader view. Here is the verse in the midst of its far-reaching context, from which we will glean the substance of what Jesus was teaching.

> For this reason I say to you, do not be anxious for your life, as to what you shall eat, or what you shall drink; nor for your body, as to what you shall put on. Is not life more than food, and the body than clothing? Look at the birds of the air, that they do not sow, neither do they reap, nor gather into barns, and yet your heavenly Father feeds them. Are you not worth much more than they? And which of you by being anxious can add a single cubit

to his life's span? And why are you anxious about clothing? Observe how the lilies of the field grow; they do not toil nor do they spin, yet I say to you that even Solomon in all his glory did not clothe himself like one of these. But if God so arrays the grass of the field, which is alive today and tomorrow is thrown into the furnace, will He not much more do so for you, O men of little faith? Do not be anxious then, saying, 'What shall we eat?' or 'What shall we drink?' or 'With what shall we clothe our-selves?' For all these things the Gentiles eagerly seek; for your heavenly Father knows that you need all these things. But seek first His kingdom and His righteousness; and all these things shall be added to you. (Matt. 6:25–33)

## ✧ God's Distributors

While it's true that we fathers are providers, we must remem-ber that we're the children of another Father and are thus being pro-vided for. God provides, so we provide. We can gather from this teaching, in concert with 1 Timothy 5:8, that we're sort of middle-men, distributors of God's loving care. As distributors, we're charged with a great responsibility, which we can best carry out by learning and applying these two important axioms. First, that God is the ultimate provider, and second, that providing sustenance is one of many vehicles for our love, not love itself. Let's look at each axiom in detail.

### *Axiom #1—God is the ultimate provider*

According to the Matthew passage, being on the receiving end of God's providing hand, as distributors, we're freed from worrying about the source of our inventory. In other words, our supplier never runs out, and His delivery channels are never blocked. God pours out His blessings twenty-four hours a day, and His tech-support line never gives a busy signal. We're to be anxious for nothing, neither food, nor drink, nor clothing. Does not God feed the birds, clothe the lilies, and array the grass of the field? Does not God, the creator who knows when a sparrow falls to the ground, also know what we need to survive?

We must understand, however, how to keep the supply channels running. In the business world, the distributor who sells effectively is the one to whom the suppliers give their priority attention. The supplier makes sure the top distributors get the best product at the best prices and that the supply lines to that distributor are always in operation. The distributor tries to impress his supplier by showing top performance, putting a larger dollar figure on the supplier's bottom line.

We don't have to worry about becoming a top distributor in order to get the best goods. God has an unlimited supply, so His best is always available. There is, however, one similarity in how God supplies us. Even though God is not impressed by salesmanship, there is a way to ensure the flow of His life-giving provision. Jesus said it in the passage above. "But seek first His kingdom and His righteousness; and all these things shall be added to you." God's provision of food, clothing, or whatever we may need is freely available to those who seek His kingdom, to those who pursue righteousness.

This point is essential. Most fathers have a clear understanding that they stand in a providing position, yet they often don't understand where the process actually begins. It doesn't begin when you sit behind the desk at the office or when you punch the clock at the construction site. It begins when you roll out of bed and ask God for guidance for the day. It continues when you whisper a word of blessing and kindness to your wife when she first opens her eyes to greet the morning. It takes another step when you awaken your children with a smile and a warm hug. It picks up steam when you read the Word of God and pray as part of your regular morning routine. It's running at full power when your five-year-old spills her juice and you patiently clean it up without a harsh word. Every act of godliness, every word of blessing, and every thought or deed that brings glory to God and His kingdom allow the channels of God's provision to flow freely.

I've learned through years of experience that God has many ways of providing, even when I can't see any of them. After more than twenty years of employment in the engineering and computer science fields, I turned from those lucrative and secure disciplines to pursue the passion of communicating God's truths through writing. Although we had no obvious means of support when I left my profession, I had full confidence that God, the boundless and unlimited provider, would sustain us, a young and growing family of nine. I knew if God was the source of the calling, He would provide the means of support. I knew as I sought after His kingdom and His righteousness, all our needs would be met. It's an exciting adventure to step out in faith and wait to see how our bountiful supplier will channel His loving flow.

## Axiom #2—Sustenance is one of many vehicles for our love, not love itself

As we provide for our families, we should remember that we're motivated by love. Some men, in their drive to succeed in their distribution channel, get caught up in the labors themselves. The thrill of accomplishment in their God-given role sometimes leads to finding satisfaction in the work that brought the excitement. A man may misinterpret the source of joy and turn his heart to the channels rather than to the ones for whom he provides. His provision becomes his only means of showing love and even becomes love itself as his fulfillment in life becomes measured by his office placement or by his influence in the boardroom. "Don't you love me?" a lonely wife cries out in despair. "I provide for you, don't I?" is the heartless answer she gets in reply.

As God numbers every hair on our heads, so are we fathers to care for the intimate details of our families' needs. We are not farmers who throw a bucket of slop in the pig trough and then sludge to the barn for the next bucket of slop. We are daddies who listen to the twittering excitement of our little ones at the dinner table, interacting with them as we answer their innocent, juvenile questions and ask questions of our own to delve into their infinitely wonderful minds. We are fathers who probe the thoughts of our older children and help them sort out the awesome complexities of growing up in a sin-sick world, addressing their new desire for autonomy as they mature, and harnessing their idealism and energy in order to channel them in God's direction. We are husbands who look deeply into the souls of our wives, searching for the silent desires of their hearts, seeking to satisfy their emotional and spiritual needs.

In all these areas, we are providers, those who distribute God's love. If we're satisfied with merely putting food on the table, we have severely undersupplied our families. We have left them hungry for provisions that are more eternally important than a loaf of bread and a bowl of soup. Millions of children all over the world are spiritually malnourished because they have fathers who cannot or will not distribute God's love beyond what a paycheck can buy.

Men, we have to look at our children as receptacles with many needs. You've probably seen recycling bins that have one hole for plastic, another for Styrofoam, and another for aluminum. Our children similarly have multiple needs. The food hole is obvious, especially for male teenagers. Their stomachs growl, and they're off to the fridge to find a way to ease their discomfort. But when our children hurt more deeply, on an emotional or spiritual level, they may not know what to do. There's no Amana side-by-side with a dozen different spiritual food choices in convenient microwaveable bowls. The spiritual input is provided through the Word of God, but our children, especially the youngest ones, may have difficulty with its deeper truths. That's where we come in.

I'm sure you've seen a mother robin feeding her nestlings. She swallows a bug or a worm and then regurgitates it for her little ones. Their constitutions are not able to take the food in its raw form, so the mother has to grind it up a bit, making it digestible. In the same way, we fathers take in the Word of God in its pure, raw form and digest it. We then teach it to our children in age-appropriate ways, helping them to understand so they can become spiritually nourished.

Once again, God is the provider, and we are the distributors, but if we're not willing to do the work necessary to maintain a proper channel, our distribution will fail. We can't simply read the Bible aloud to our children and expect them to understand it, though by God's grace and mercy they will likely glean some measure of its truths. Instead, as we take in the Word ourselves, as we're made holy by following its precepts, as we learn to explain it clearly because we truly understand it, then our children will gladly take it in.

Teaching a powerful gospel that has made us into holy men in the strength of the Lord is like telling our children to eat vegetables while we flex our biceps to show them what that awesome broccoli did for us. Our spiritual character will shine forth, making our words desirable, and our understanding and communication will be clear, making our words digestible. In this way, our children will eagerly seek us out to satisfy the spiritual craving that growls like a hungry stomach.

## ✧ Where Is Your Heart?

Our workaday labors are means to an end, not the end itself. Our jobs are neither our identity nor our passion. If we have to work outside of our homes, we leave home, where we find our identities, in order to perform a duty. Yes, we'll have friendships and camaraderie at our places of employment, but those relationships should be secondary to the bond we share with those at home, where we left our hearts when we walked out the door. Our return at the end of our hours of labor is a true homecoming every day. Our smiles should be a genuine reflection of the joy of returning to the delights of our heart, our cherished wife and children.

My wife, Susie, purposefully trained our children to greet me warmly each day as I returned home, regardless of what kind of day they had. The younger children, Rachel and Hannah, ran to grab my legs before I could even get completely out of the car. They hung on tightly, cheerily singing out "Daddy's home! Daddy's home!" Then I took two pairs of reaching arms and hoisted them into my own, carrying a couple of bundles of supercharged welcome wagons into the house. The older children were not quite as demonstrative, but they did welcome me with genuine gladness.

Although Susie did the at-home training, I was the key to making all this happen. It was my job to make them glad I had come home. I, too, expressed heartfelt words of happiness that I had arrived. I asked them questions about their day, read a book to a toddler, dashed into the yard for Frisbee throwing or welcomed whatever interaction they needed to help them know that I brought home my love and care for them. To plop myself in front of the television in order to "unwind" was out of the question. The frustrations of my day and my tight ball of nerves from the busy, hectic hours on the job were wondrously unraveled in the joy of being with Susie and our children, interacting with those with whom I had left my heart earlier that day.

The substance of our lesson boils down to the teaching of Jesus, once again in Matthew chapter 6. "For where your treasure is, there will your heart be also" (verse 21). Fathers, where is your treasure? Where do you find what you value most? Is it at your place of employment, or is it at home? If you find this question difficult to answer, ask yourself where you would rather be. With whom do you most wish to spend time? Where do you find satisfaction and fulfillment? If your answer is at work, then you have some soul-searching to do, and you probably already know that a serious problem threatens the survival of your family.

How do we find treasure at home? The answer begins with us. Delving into this subject completely is beyond the scope of this book, but we can get a start by briefly looking back at the principle we highlighted earlier. Seek first God's kingdom and His righteousness, and all these things shall be added to you. In order to train our minds to focus on what God desires, we have to know what God values, what He considers treasure. It's not the pride of accomplishment, or the bulge in a wallet; it's purely and simply love—selfless, giving, unconditional love. If our priorities, our views on what is valuable, are flip-flopped, then we need to faithfully and seriously study the Word of God and experience His ways—how He loved even a sinful and rebellious people so much that He gave His only Son as a sacrificial lamb to be beaten, scourged, and brutally crucified.

This is love. This is our model. We are to be men so committed to the spiritual welfare of our families that we would gladly suffer and die to bring about their salvation. If we demonstrate by our actions that our treasure lies in wealth and achievement, then our children will follow in our footsteps and live by the same priority. If we live a lie, they will not believe our words, whether we teach the Bible or not. For where our treasure is, there will our children's hearts be also.

Our sacrifice may begin by giving up certain pleasures in life. Television watching is a luxury that steals precious hours from your family, rarely returning value for the time investment it demands. Ignoring the alarm clock or banging its snooze button to get that extra few minutes of sleep may seem like a minor indulgence, but it can rob you of the crucial few minutes with God that a less hectic morning can provide. And just fifteen morning minutes is enough for a round of blood-pumping exercise that can fill your body with life-charging energy, making you ready to face the challenges of the day.

Our sacrifices continue as we look for positive ways to serve our families. We are to set our minds in one direction, to serve. As Jesus said, "The Son of Man did not come to be served, but to serve, and to give His life a ransom for many" (Matt. 20:28). If Jesus, the Holy One of God, through Whom all things were created, was willing to be a servant, then shouldn't we be willing also? Yes, we can still be leaders in our homes, but we are to follow the example of Christ, Who, being the husband of His bride, the church, willingly gave everything for her salvation, for her holiness, and for her future eternal home in heaven.

The smallest servant deeds can work wonders. Make the bed. Get up early and prepare breakfast for everyone. Do the laundry once a month. And always open the door for your dear wife. Show her the chivalrous courtesies that demonstrate your view of her as a cherished and deserving lady, not only when the two of you are alone, but also in front of your children. We are to be living sacrifices, showing in our bodies the sacrifice of Christ and making our provision of the gospel a beautiful and desired treasure.

So, we're the breadwinners, channeling God's provision to those whom He has given us, but the bread isn't just biscuits and buns; it's also the bread of life, Jesus, the Word of God. As Jesus said, "For what does it profit a man to gain the whole world, and forfeit his soul?" (Mark 8:36). In the same way, what good is it if we feed our children a loaf of bread, yet they starve for the true bread that could give them life eternal? While filling their bellies, we would leave their souls ravenous, and they would be forced to search for nourishment in foreign places, provided through channels other than God's own.

Jesus said, "I am the bread of life; he who comes to Me shall not hunger, and he who believes in Me shall never thirst" (John 6:35). Let us ever give this bread to our children and sate that spiritual gnawing, filling the void so it never goes wanting again.

## ✧ Summary

God is the ultimate provider for our families, and we are the distributors, carefully nurturing the channels God uses to pour forth what we need. We have no reason to be anxious, because God loves us and has an unlimited supply of whatever we need. The channels of God's provision are opened and maintained through our seeking after His kingdom and righteousness as we bestow His love on others.

While we understand our role as earthly providers, we see that role as multi-faceted, with physical and spiritual faces. Our jobs are our means of provision, vehicles for our love, not love itself. We don't find our ultimate satisfaction and fulfillment in our employment, for that's simply one of the facets in our role as provider. Our treasures and our hearts are firmly housed in our families, at home, and only by learning to understand and obeying God's heart through His words are we able to find our real treasure.

3

# The Father as Comforter

## ✧ We Have Been There

Fear of the unknown surrounds the young; strange shapes in the darkness, creepy sounds in the night, slithering creatures under the bed or in the closet. They all work together to make little hands clench the sheets and yank them over their heads until dawn of the next day. Even the worries of the world—political unrest, wars, street crime, and kidnappings—can deeply disturb young minds. They hear the news and imagine the troubles sneaking into their own homes; they magnify the dangers, exaggerating them, having no experience to discern the real risks.

As Christian fathers we realize there is no need for fear. We agree with King David, "Even though I walk through the valley of the shadow of death, I fear no evil; for Thou art with me; Thy rod and Thy staff, they comfort me" (Ps. 23:4). We know that our heavenly Father is a God of comfort as the apostle Paul so clearly taught. "Blessed be the God and Father of our Lord Jesus Christ, the Father of mercies and God of all comfort; who comforts us in all our affliction so that we may be able to comfort those who are in any affliction with the comfort with which we ourselves are comforted by God" (2 Cor. 1:3, 4).

From this passage, we learn without a doubt that we're to reflect God's comforting ways, passing His comfort on to our children. It is through knowing God, experiencing His comfort through our own trials, remembering His mercies when we wondered about the future, seeing His mighty works when we could not see how the days of trouble would end, that we have the confidence to stand now without fear.

Our children don't have that luxury. They may not have seen a mighty God march like the commander of a great army to save you from a dangerous predicament. Perhaps they weren't there when God's healing hand touched a friend of yours and brought him back from the brink of death. With few exceptions, they've never faced a fierce enemy and experienced deliverance from his evil intent. But if you've been a Christian for more than a few years, especially if you've done mission work on the gospel frontiers, then you have been there. You have seen God's powerful hand move to thwart your enemies. You have felt His loving arms wrap around you in the midst of alarm. You have heard of His mighty deeds from brothers and sisters all over the world who have escaped the wiles of Satan, the crafty liar who would seek to stop the spread of the gospel.

As those who have seen and heard the works of God, we have experienced His comforting touch. It's our duty, therefore, to extend that comfort to our little ones, so they, too, may feel the warm blanket of protection when they suffer the chill of the unknown. There are two ways we as fathers can reflect the comfort God has extended to us: (1) by telling our children about God's great works, and (2) by living our lives in complete confidence in God's care for us. These two go hand in hand and cannot be separated. We'll look at each in detail and then merge them into one important application.

## ✧ Telling of God's Mercies

Whether or not monsters really stalk the minds of our children from the dark corners of their rooms, tales of God's protection will help them stare down the murky shadows, and they'll sleep, heads uncovered, in blissful confidence and peace. As we consider what stories to tell, we can look to the Scriptures for our guidelines. In the book of Deuteronomy we find a specific instance in which God directs us to relate His mighty works.

> When your son asks you in time to come, saying, "What do the testimonies and the statutes and the judgments mean which the Lord our God commanded you?" then you shall say to your son, "We were slaves to Pharaoh in Egypt; and the Lord brought us from Egypt with a mighty hand. Moreover, the Lord showed great and distressing signs and wonders before our eyes against Egypt, Pharaoh and all his household; and He brought us out from there in order to bring us in, to give us the land which He had sworn to our fathers." (Deut. 6:20–23)

Notice that the story of God's mighty hand was offered in response to a question about the meaning of God's laws. The father was to explain to his son how God led His people, showed great signs, and established their home. But there was a specific motivation in mind, and the rest of the passage reveals it.

So the Lord commanded us to observe all these statutes, to fear the Lord our God for our good always and for our survival, as it is today. And it will be righteousness for us if we are careful to observe all this commandment before the Lord our God, just as He commanded us. (Deut. 6:24, 25)

It is obedience to God's Word that ensures His protective hand. Our observance of His statutes is for our good, for our survival. Our confidence in God's comfort is fortified when we're also confident in our working out the righteousness He has bestowed on us. And a story about God's protection seems incomplete, a tale without a moral, unless we relate that we can't expect such merciful acts if we're not walking in His ways.

It is true that God sometimes rescues wayward souls. He is merciful and full of grace, having patience and loving-kindness throughout the generations. Yet, we're called not to test that grace, but to confirm it, establishing His holy character in ourselves, the ones to whom He extends His comforting support.

So what stories do we tell? What kind of tale would help our children see the light of God's protection even in the darkest of times, something that would compare to what the Israelites experienced? They were able to recount the horrible plagues God used to smash the pride of the Egyptian monarch, the parting of a sea that threatened to hem them in against the thundering chariots and the points of sharpened spears, and the conquering of terrifying giants who occupied the fruitful land God had promised. What could compare to those stories of awesome might?

At our home we receive mission magazines, and we delight in reading the stories of our dedicated missionaries in foreign and often dangerous countries. Whether at the dinner table or during our evening devotions, I enjoy watching the wide eyes of the younger children as we recount the dangers, even near-fatal encounters, from which God has rescued countless numbers of His servants. Of course there are times when God chooses to allow some of His faithful ones to go home to heaven, but even then we emphasize that they've gone to a place of comfort, reaching the end of their earthly ministry as faithful soldiers of Christ. We can even rejoice with them. How great is the joy to die in the midst of service to God! Even stories like these bring comfort as the children picture a powerful angel escorting a martyr into a joyous "Welcome Home" celebration.

Along with sharing the stories of others, I frequently sprinkle in my own recollections. Some of God's works in my life are quite impressive, and I enjoy glorifying the Lord by sharing those situations with my children. And it doesn't hurt to tell them the same story more than once, for the effect it has on their hearts changes over the years as each child matures in wisdom and understanding. Stories that may seem "small," God's little mercies on a day-to-day basis, help our children see God's intimate care, that He is not just concerned about the big issues—war, disease, and parting seas—He truly does care for us more than the sparrows He counts in the fields. I tell them about the near miss on the highway, about how a stranger hailed me and gave me the wallet I had just dropped, and about an edifying e-mail from a Christian friend. I also encourage them to tell me about their activities, so we try to identify the events in which we can see God's protection and resulting comfort.

Sometimes stories of faraway lands and recollections of times long past may not soothe a child who senses a closer, more present danger. Perhaps he's experiencing a situation no story can address. Although you may unsuccessfully rack your brain to come up with a memory that parallels his troubling circumstance, there's still a way to help your child find comfort. We don't have to rely on a specific event God has already handled; we can rely on the immovable foundation of God's character, the unsearchable depths of His wisdom, and the inestimable reach of His power. Simply put, there's nothing God can't handle, and this simple message brings comfort to almost any child. But there is one caveat—you have to live like you believe it; and we'll cover that issue next.

## ✧ Living with Confidence

Talk is cheap, so says the old cliché. And its truth is undeniable. Who cares about a person's words if his actions don't match up? If we merely tell stories about God's great works and we don't live like we believe them, we're showing our children bald-face hypocrisy. By our actions we tell them we don't believe the stories, so why should they?

When children hear of dangers in their own neighborhood or even in their town, whether from criminals or weather emergencies, the worst thing they can see is a father who appears nervous about the situation. They should see you prepare for an emergency, whether it be to lock the doors, board up the windows, or cut down low hanging branches in the yard. In fact, seeing you working hard to protect them will enhance any comfort you try to extend. If, however, they see you pace the floor, glance nervously around the room, or become distracted by the anxious events of the day, your lack of confidence will spread to them like a contagion and become multiplied in their hearts.

Whenever danger seems near, it's a good time to sing a song or even dance. As the Bible says,

> Then the virgin shall rejoice in the dance,
> And the young men and the old, together,
> For I will turn their mourning into joy,
> And will comfort them, and give them joy for their sorrow.
>     (Jer. 31:13)

Indeed, the Lord will comfort Zion;
He will comfort all her waste places.
And her wilderness He will make like Eden,
And her desert like the garden of the Lord;
Joy and gladness will be found in her,
Thanksgiving and sound of a melody. (Isa. 51:3)

The act of joyous singing and dancing is not only a sign that we've cast our cares on a great God who loves us, it actually works to set our hearts at peace as we rejoice in His goodness and might.

We are to be pictures of confidence, showing our lack of worry in our speech, our facial expressions, and our daily activities. Even in troubling times we should laugh and sing, sharing hugs and smiles, for we trust in God, whatever the end of the trial should bring. We know that, for a believer, even death brings more comfort and joy than we could ever imagine.

We are to be like Moses when the Egyptians pursued the Hebrews to the edge of the Red Sea. As the roar of battle approached and the dust of charging horses rose into the sky on the horizon, the hearts of the people of Israel melted. The frightened mass turned against their leader, saying, "Is it because there were no graves in Egypt that you have taken us away to die in the wilderness? Why have you dealt with us in this way, bringing us out of Egypt?" (Exod. 14:11). But Moses said to the people, "Do not fear! Stand by and see the salvation of the Lord which He will accomplish for you today; for the Egyptians whom you have seen today, you will never see them again forever. The Lord will fight for you while you keep silent" (Exod. 14:13, 14). Such was the confidence of this man of God who sought to comfort the people through his own steadfast faith.

The apostle Paul stands as another example of bravery, exhibiting the courage that brings comfort to those less stalwart. We find this story in the book of Acts.

A certain prophet named Agabus came down from Judea. And coming to us, he took Paul's belt and bound his own feet and hands, and said, "This is what the Holy Spirit says: 'In this way the Jews at Jerusalem will bind the man who owns this belt and deliver him into the hands of the Gentiles.'" And when we had heard this, we as well as the local residents began begging him not to go up to Jerusalem. (Acts 21:10–12)

Paul's answer proved his faith in God's ever-present protection.

Then Paul answered, "What are you doing, weeping and breaking my heart? For I am ready not only to be bound, but even to die at Jerusalem for the name of the Lord Jesus." And since he would not be persuaded, we fell silent, remarking, "The will of the Lord be done!" (Acts 21:13, 14)

It's said that Stonewall Jackson, confederate general in the American Civil War, would walk his horse slowly along the front lines, sitting straight and without a hint of fear, though bullets and cannon fired all about him and lead balls nicked his coat and boots in the midst of the deadly hail. The soldiers would see him either lifting his hands in prayer with his eyes toward heaven or comforting his troops as his horse clopped along the line. He would speak softly, saying, "All's well, all's well." His example of taking a real stand of faith moved the hearts of his men from trembling in their trenches to charging fearlessly onto the battlefields.

We are to live by the examples of these leaders, showing true and honest faith in God's protective hand. This is the image of a father, a man who stands courageously in the midst of danger, spreading his heaven-born tranquility to his children who may otherwise sit shivering in fear. They know their father's character has been chiseled by the hand of God. They feed from his brimming confidence, believing that even if he should fall into the hands of his enemies, he would be caught in the hands of his Savior.

Fathers, this is the true test, the test of fire. If we fail to show courage, we'll be to our children no more than a set of empty words, men who talk a good talk but don't really believe our own tongues. Should we pass the great test, however, we'll be living lights, not only proving God's word in the hearts of our children forever; we'll bring comfort that lasts for more years than we can imagine, as the story of our stand in the darkest of days is told for generations to come.

## ✦ Making Home a Place of Comfort

We can tell wondrous stories of God's saving works and live as believers in His comforting protective hand, but if we don't combine the two in one crucial application, all our efforts will be for naught.

The most precious gift of comfort a father can give his children is a stable home. I'm not talking about maintaining a house that doesn't collapse. That's important, but damage to your house is repairable. I'm talking about your relationship with your wife. Nothing is more traumatic to a child than to see his mother and father fighting. That kind of dispute signals the scariest of instabilities, and avoiding it is essential.

Children of divorced parents learn to cope with their tragedy, but rarely do they recover from the devastation wrought on their sense of security. The most important picture of God's love for His people, the cleaving of one flesh to another, has been torn asunder. How can a child have trust after his comfort has been shattered? How can he believe in anyone's word after the most holy vow has been cast aside like a trite cliché? What story of God's mighty works will he believe? Who will comfort him now?

Our children see the results of divorce all around them—classmates or friends who have no respect for authority because their faith in great institutions has been throttled at its foundations. These young victims of divorce can't believe anything when they see their parents, the ones whom they trusted most, have broken a sacred vow. If they can't be trusted, who can?

When we moved into Baltimore's inner city, Susie and I had been married only about five months. On our short block we counted about thirty children, only three of whom lived with both parents. The others lived with single moms, grandparents, or aunts and uncles. Divorce was certainly rampant in the Waverly district just southwest of Memorial Stadium. On one occasion, while getting to know a couple of little girls who lived nearby, Susie and I chatted with them, mostly small talk about school and family. Being young and inexperienced, we were shocked when one of the girls asked, "So, when are you getting divorced?"

Stunned for a few seconds, I could only come up with a simple reply of faith. "Why, we're never getting divorced. We took a vow to stay together forever."

"Oh, you'll get divorced," came the sad but serious reply. "Everyone does."

I'll never forget her eyes, somber, yet cold; searching, yet with a wall of protection built up to keep her feelings in and trust in anyone else out.

This widespread lack of trust can foster fear in our own children. *Could I be next?* they may wonder. *Could my parents somehow split up?* With the divorce rate so high, even among people in the church, who can blame them for thinking terrifying thoughts like these?

We can thwart these fears by demonstrating to our children the true covenant of marriage—two parents who are fused as one unbreakable unit. Make this vow and keep it: Not only will my children never witness the evil specter of divorce in our home, I will give them no reason to even sense its threat. The word will never be uttered as an option, nor will it ever enter my mind. They'll never even hear a cross word between my wife and me, such will be our holy oneness.

A fight between husband and wife is like a madman cutting himself, his insanity driving him to self-harm; and divorce is like suicide, the last desperate act of a mind so diseased it can no longer stand to visit another day of thought.

There is no problem, no threat, no crisis so large that can force a husband and wife to be at odds with one another. Instead, every day draws a true Christian husband and wife closer, binding them so inseparably that they begin to even think as one. Remember, as Jesus loves the church, so should we men love our wives, and the result will be children who live in comfort, secure that there's one visual covenant upon which they can rely, their wedded parents.

## ✧ My Father, My Comfort

A father is responsible for demonstrating strength, giving hope to family members who rely on his courage and showing tenderness and compassion toward children who might tremble in fear at the shadows of the night. He provides comfort, both by living a life that gives a child reason to trust, as we have already seen in this chapter, and also by speaking words of grace.

God is surely a warrior who shouts, commanding a legion of angelic troops who stand ready to protect us in our need. Yet He also whispers words of comfort, as He did to quiet Elijah's quaking heart, speaking in a gentle wind rather than in an earthquake or a fire (see 1 Kings 19:12).

A father's gentle touch—a soft hand on his daughter's cheek or on his son's shoulder—penetrates deeply, radiating warmth through young hearts and minds. A word whispered quietly is heard more distinctly and remembered far longer than any robust shout. A bedtime prayer with its quiet murmurings of faith, spoken in a father's gentle hum, will loosen tight eyelids and calm twitching little bodies, especially when sealed with a soft, masculine kiss on the forehead.

As fathers we find it more natural to show our strength, our male hormones flowing to give us flexing biceps and aroused bravery. But never underestimate the tremendous power of a tender touch, the blessed calm that follows a soothing whisper. When a man who exudes strength and courage, wielding a mighty sword in his muscular arms, is so assured of God's protection that he can kneel to pet his little lambs, this brings peace and long-lasting comfort beyond any battle story a man can invent. And, not only that, the little lambs will forever realize the powerful shepherd is always on their side.

Fathers, our children see us as the hand of God, an extension of His comforting grace. Let us not forget to reflect all the attributes of His protective hand.

### A Fear for the Night, a Knight for the Fear

I prayed the Lord my soul to keep
While laying down my head to sleep.
But there was a part I was scared to pray;
"If I should die," I could not say.

When I'm all alone, I don't feel so bold.
I don't want to die. I'm not even old.
I want to go run and roll in the grass
Play fetch with my dog and go fishing for bass.

I saw on the news; there's coming a storm.
It knocked down some houses and a big college dorm.
You think it could come here, a big mean ol' twister?
O God, please protect my Mom and my sister.

I hear the strong wind, and it's dark in my room.
The storm's getting started; the thunder goes boom.
It's getting so loud, it sounds like a bomb,
But I'm getting too big to go running to Mom.

My Dad's gone to England, or was it Japan?
He'll be home tomorrow; at least that was the plan.
But what if that storm pulls his plane from the sky?
Could it be somehow that my Daddy could die?

I wish that my Daddy had come home today
To catch all my fears and chase them away.
But instead I hear scratching, a groan, and a thump;
My heart starts to pound and my throat has a lump.

Were the sounds from my closet or under my bed?
I'll pull all the covers up over my head
And poke out my nose to get some fresh air.
This way I'll hide from whatever's out there.

And now the wind's howling; the rain starts its beating;
I hear a door slam, some footsteps and breathing.
I pull my sheets tighter and cover my nose;
I feel full of shivers from my head to my toes.

Then a deep voice and a hand on my head
End my night terrors, my fears and my dread.
"Father" it sings in a whisper and prayer,
"Thank you for watching my family with care."

He pulls my sheet down and I feel his soft lips;
I smell my Dad's smell, and his soggy hair drips,
I pretend not to notice when the rain tickles my chin.
With a manner so loving he tucks me back in.

He walks to my sister and kisses her too;
I hear his wet clothes and the squeak of his shoe.
He tries to be quiet, softly closing the door,
The squeaks are like music as he walks the hall floor.

The storm rages on with lightning and thunder.
It still makes me shiver; it still makes me wonder,
But now I don't fear and my mind doesn't roam;
I can sleep tight now 'cause my Daddy's come home.

—BRYAN DAVIS

## ✧ Summary

As Christian fathers we've had years of experiencing God's protective grace, a benefit our children haven't yet received. It's important that we recount stories of rescues and triumphs that wouldn't have happened had not God intervened in some way. These stories can come from our own memory archives or from other sources, such as missionary magazines, Christian biographies, or, obviously, from the Bible itself.

We are also called to live out the confidence we teach, not allowing the tide of onrushing danger to affect our courage or countenance. We can prepare for the perils we might perceive, but we mustn't allow fear to hold sway. We can shoo it away with songs of praise and carefree dancing unto the Lord.

We are to make our homes places of comfort, demonstrating to our children the steadfast, immovable bond between husband and wife, living a true oneness of flesh that can never be separated. Such a solid rock will allow our children to stand on our promises, giving them comfort that they will always have a visible sign of God's covenantal love.

Finally, we fathers are called to show God's tenderness through soothing speech and gentle hands. When the children's powerful protector displays his confidence with warmth and grace, peace reigns in that man's household. The children feel safe, knowing that the man who wields the sword of God is on their side.

# The Father as Teacher

## ✧ Heart Teaching

"Walk fast," the teacher barked.

I couldn't believe how fast he was walking. Being in his late sixties, he wasn't a great physical specimen, gray-haired, a bit overweight, yet quick and mobile, speed walking up and down the halls of Avon Park High School. I looked at the note, handwritten in Mr. Burns's distinct brand of capital letters. It read, "CWM. IWTSYS." After many months under his tutelage I had learned how to quickly translate his queer notes. "Come with me," it said, "I want to show you something." And "Come with me," also meant, "Walk fast." Otherwise, I would be left behind. *If Mr. Burns wants to show me something,* I thought, *it's worth seeing.* So I would trot behind, drafting in his wake, as I anticipated the upcoming adventure with my favorite teacher.

I have fond memories of my experiences with Mr. Frank Burns. At times he was abrupt, though I knew it was an act, the merry gleam in his eye giving away his mirth. Some parents wondered at how so many students could be enamored with such a man, a puzzling former mining engineer who smoked rather heavily, employed an unorthodox teaching style, and often displayed an acerbic attitude. Many parents were baffled at why their normally apathetic children were so determined to perform well in his classes. During my years in high school, while I was absorbing his lessons, even at the expense of other classes, I don't think I could have explained it either. Now, as I look back fondly on those years, I think I know the answer.

Before I could drive, Mr. Burns would pick me up at 6:15 in the morning, and I'd join a few other students in his science classroom for our 6:30 Club meeting, where we'd finish homework, study for a test, and yak about the goings-on at school. Since the first bell didn't sound until 8:00 A.M., we were considered quite strange for wanting to show up so early in the morning. But Mr. Burns encouraged us to be different. He certainly was different, and he had the respect, if not the friendship, of every teacher in school.

Mr. Burns taught using a method he called "Recency and Frequency," meaning he would require us to repeat our recitations throughout the school year. We knew that a question from an early lesson could show up on a test weeks or even months later, and he drilled us in class until every student knew the concepts forward and backward. To this day I can still recite Newton's Law of Universal Gravitation, list Moh's Scale of Hardness, and identify numerous rocks and minerals. His methods worked.

Even with his gruff exterior, Mr. Burns showed compassion. I remember a particular student who was mentally disabled and declared by the other teachers to be uncontrollable. Mr. Burns volunteered to teach him, taking him during every class period, making him a teaching assistant of sorts. He would handle laboratory stock, distribute and collect papers, and clean up messes. I'll never forget how Mr. Burns would send this boy to get coffee. He purposefully gave him too much money. When the boy returned he had to give an account of the price and how the change was calculated. After just a few months, everyone was amazed at the transformation in this formerly incorrigible boy. He was learning!

I relate these memories not because Frank Burns was a model all teachers should emulate but to show that the hearts and minds of young people can be captured and molded by a man who strives to reach them with more than just an academic strategy. Mr. Burns pursued our hearts and made us want to learn.

How many stories have we heard about sports coaches who have inspired ordinary kids to win championships or music teachers who have coaxed greatness out of the mundane? Almost without exception, their successes lie in reaching for the hearts of their pupils, not just their heads. Unfortunately, this maxim holds true for evil as well, for many cult leaders have ensnared young minds by appealing to more than just the intellect in their pursuit of adherents.

Our ultimate teacher, God our Father, was the first to employ this method of "Heart Teaching." God doesn't want us to learn His precepts just so we can glibly recite them when called upon; He wants our hearts, stoked by refining firebrands and burning with impassioned heat for His glory.

> Then the Lord said, "Because this people draw near with their
>> words
> And honor Me with their lip service,
> But they remove their hearts far from Me,
> And their reverence for Me consists of tradition learned by rote,
> Therefore behold, I will once again deal marvelously with this
>> people, wondrously marvelous;

And the wisdom of their wise men shall perish,
And the discernment of their discerning men shall be concealed."
    (Isa. 29:13, 14)

Teaching has long been considered a profession that distributes information and then tests the student to determine whether or not that information has been learned. It's traditionally a brain-centered pursuit, measured by IQ scores from multiple-choice tests and an essay or two. The desk dwellers are force-fed books full of information and are expected to neatly regurgitate it all at the end of the term. They're treated as clones, reviewed and graded using standardized tests formulated by people who barely know their names and who know nothing about their hearts. Most students are able to perform in robotic response, some barely survive the boredom, and a few fail, unable to grasp the value of a discipline so bound up in intellectual monotony. The students then grow up and teach their little ones in the same manner, educating their minds but not capturing their hearts, creating a legacy of generations who learn by rote and honor their professors with lip service. This is not Heart Teaching.

## ✧ Blended, Not Separated—A Father's Teaching Responsibility

It's up to fathers to reflect the image of God the Teacher, the holy pursuer of the hearts of men. God knows our hearts intimately. He is able to create individualized paths on which our feet would best walk, and He teaches us based on what we need to know, when we need to know it. He intermixes intellectual understanding with the spiritual reasons that lie behind and support the physical observations.

Consider the lilies, how they grow; they neither toil nor spin; but I tell you, even Solomon in all his glory did not clothe himself like one of these. But if God so arrays the grass in the field, which is alive today and tomorrow is thrown into the furnace, how much more will He clothe you, O men of little faith! (Luke 12:27, 28)

For since the creation of the world His invisible attributes, His eternal power and divine nature, have been clearly seen, being understood through what has been made. (Rom. 1:20)

With our own precious children, we're compelled to follow God's model, to fit our children for God's service through diligent, even dogged, pursuit of their hearts. We should train them with the proper perspective in mind—that every laboratory proof, every historical event, and every mathematical formula has its origin in God and exists for God's glory.

Fathers, as reflectors of God's teaching heart, we establish for our children the synergy of academic and spiritual instruction. Through observation and God-given wisdom, we collate data from external sources and weave a cohesive tapestry, showing how all of creation glorifies God. But too many have declined their obligation, relying instead on others without exercising proper consideration or oversight. Why is this so?

Some fathers separate teaching responsibilities into neatly defined categories and hire the appropriate professionals to handle each one. The secular teacher handles observable disciplines, the academics; and the cleric, whether a pastor or a Sunday school teacher, takes care of spiritual lessons. If a father chooses this route, he may consider his job complete. He may believe he has seen to both major aspects of education for his children and not pursue it any further. Unfortunately, this parentally endorsed separation of church and state encourages a compartmentalized way of thinking. It encourages an opposition between heart and mind. It sets science and spirit at odds rather than blending them in cooperation.

While it is allowable, and sometimes even preferable, to send a child to a professional teacher, overseeing a child's education is a father's job. No one else can better reflect his heavenly Father's pursuit of heart and mind and tailor a learning program for his beloved children. A father formulates a plan that will point to God and give Him the glory for every facet of His awe-inspiring creation. A father blends the academic with the spiritual; he unites science and spirit. He collects various inputs from teachers, pastors, and books, and shows his children how it all points to God as the ultimate source of truth.

Having a professional educator for your children is not the end of your educational responsibility. An outside teacher is a hired hand who supplements the home-based educational engine, the place where a father carefully guides intake and outflow, making sure his children are fed a balanced educational meal that produces God-centered minds.

## Laying Down the Path

Many of us have heard over and over, "Train up a child in the way he should go, even when he is old he will not depart from it" (Prov. 22:6). This is a great truth, and the Bible expands on that thought in Psalm 78.

> Listen, O my people, to my instruction;
> Incline your ears to the words of my mouth.
> I will open my mouth in a parable;
> I will utter dark sayings of old,
> Which we have heard and known,
> And our fathers have told us.
> We will not conceal them from their children,
> But tell to the generation to come the praises of the Lord,
> And His strength and His wondrous works that He has done.
> For He established a testimony in Jacob,
> And appointed a law in Israel,
> Which He commanded our fathers,

That they should teach them to their children,
That the generation to come might know, even the children yet
　　to be born,
That they may arise and tell them to their children,
That they should put their confidence in God,
And not forget the works of God,
But keep His commandments,
And not be like their fathers,
A stubborn and rebellious generation,
A generation that did not prepare its heart,
And whose spirit was not faithful to God. (Ps. 78:1–8)

What we impart to our children has first been imparted to us. The "sayings of old" are not merely tattered poems from a faded generation; they are sacred truths, which have been lovingly passed down to us by someone who cared enough to reveal them, repeat them, and record them for those who would remain after their earthly departure. If we fathers do not pass along such a great legacy, then the chain of spiritual inheritance will be broken. How can the children who are yet to be born discover the true beauty of the lilies of the field except they learn it from someone who knows? How else can they see God's attributes, His detailed forethought and careful design in the structure of the eye or the pollinating legs of a bee?

We want our children to have a clear path, one so unmistakably true that departing from it would seem ridiculous even during a crisis, even when others dispute its usefulness. The path is eternal. It was laid before we were born, and it will go on after we leave. Our children will follow it if we prove that it's trustworthy, that it can stand up to any test.

A hired teacher will not establish that path for them; she cannot know where it began or where it leads. She is merely a helper who provides raw material for its construction. A father takes that material and puts it in its proper perspective. He knows the sayings of old, and he knows God's promises for the future. He considers the lilies and describes for his children God's attention to beauty and His illustration of the frailty of life. He takes a diagram of the eye and points to a great designer who knows we have a need to see what lies in front of us. As a father unites the observable with the invisible, he creates the sublime, a path that can be trusted in every generation.

Our diligence in overseeing our children's education will produce a priceless treasure. They will put their confidence in God and not forget His works, because we valued them enough to hand them down. They will keep His commandments because they will see Him for who He really is, believe Him because they see His hand in the lilies, exalt Him because the wonder of their physical eyes enthralls their spiritual vision, and trust Him because they feel His loving care in the passing down of a blessed legacy.

## Maintaining the Path

"Train up a child in the way he should go, even when he is old he will not depart from it." Is the proverb always true or is it just a general statement of principle? Do some children depart from the path in which they should walk even after being trained properly? Why does a child sometimes depart from the way he should go? From my experience, one reason is clear; he or she was exposed to influences that countered and overcame what was taught at home. Maybe it was a charismatic professor who captured the heart of a college-aged man, or a book filled with persuasive arguments that swayed a youth who had never previously encountered its philosophy. Whatever the influence, a child needs to be prepared to face the onslaught of conflicting ideas that is sure to come. Training a child in the way he should go must include establishing defenses against forces that would lure him from the path of truth.

We know that the most important part of a house is its foundation. Almost any other structural problem can be repaired, but a faulty foundation requires that a house be completely rebuilt. Similarly, the foundational quality of a young person's path defines the ground on which he walks. Can he trust it to be firm, to lead him to a good end? Though there may be many dangers on the road, if the road itself is trustworthy, a young person may be encouraged to continue no matter how difficult the effort of traveling on God's path becomes.

The firm ground upon which we stand and with which we build a path for our children is the truth of God's Word, made firm by the trustworthiness of God's revealed character and by the simple logical consistency of God's proclamations. The myriad doctrines that are built upon the foundation may be useful, but they can never replace the firmness of the most basic tenets of the faith. That's why, when my children ponder difficult questions, even those that use scientific claims for evidence, I always bring them back to basic, undeniable truths; the necessity of God's existence and a host of proofs of creation. Once those foundations are again established in their minds, their paths regain a firm feel, and the specific challenges can be addressed in order. After answering every question as thoroughly as I can, I then try to point out the sandy soil on which modern thought finds its footing. I ask a series of questions of my own.

How many times have scientists changed their minds? How often have pet theories been dashed by further research, even by the scientists who framed them? I assure my children that the latest contradiction of God's truths will pass just like the ones before it. Darwin's theories of evolution are under attack even by former Darwinists, archeologists continue to discover lost biblical civilizations they thought never really existed, Big Bang apologists still get red faces when asked where the explosion came from. This is part of the legacy; God's truth never fails. Attacks against its unerring qualities never pass the test of time or logic. God always wins, and we need to be sure our kids know they can count on Him.

The key to path maintenance is knowing where to shore up the soft spots and identifying any holes that need to be repaired. In other words, communication has to remain open; our children need to feel free to bring us their questions. As they get older, their desire to present their queries may diminish as we become less accessible for one reason or another. That's why part of their training is to make them feel comfortable enough to raise any issue, any doubt or concern, no matter how difficult or trivial. We might even raise possible questions ourselves, the kinds of challenges we've heard in our own experience. These can be discussed, multiple times if necessary, to be sure our children are well equipped, not only to defend against a current challenge, but also to fend off future ones.

One of my favorite places to create a challenge encounter is at the dinner table. After a day of work, school, or recreation, it's natural to discuss the news of the day at the evening meal. I often try to interject a question about the relevance of some news event or personal happening to stimulate conversation. Frequently we'll break down the mundane event into its underlying motivations, the desires of men's hearts, and perhaps God's purpose in allowing it to happen. These encounters train my children to think and challenge them to analyze what lies beneath the surface. As they learn to see more than what others might see, they grow confident not only in their own cognitive abilities but also in those of their father. As time goes on, they watch the truth unfold as the details of a news event are revealed. Many times we've witnessed our hypotheses proven true as what was hidden in the background is brought to light.

We've discussed politics, predicting the actions of government leaders and how their motivations are often based on political expediency rather than ethics. We debate interpersonal issues, trying to determine motivations of acquaintances as we decide whether or not to continue a relationship or pursue closer friendship. We even find fruitful discussion in sports, evaluating role models, examining the function of athletics in a well-balanced life, and predicting the actions of certain coaches based on our perception of their moral standing. As our solid foundation of truth emerges as a trust-worthy and prophetic voice, our children gain confidence in its practical value.

Confidence is crucial. In order for our children to consider coming back to us with questions, they have to trust that we either have the answers or that we can help them find the answers. Our children need a good reason to make the effort to ask rather than just assume that the academics who challenge their faith are correct. Are you a source of reason, having proven yourself as a champion of truth and a warrior in the battlefield of ideas, able to skillfully wield the sword of sound logic? Are you well versed in God's Word, ready to defend what it really means and to live according to its precepts?

Fathers, this is your job as the primary teacher of your children. The professionals will eventually fade away. Sooner or later the paid instructor will retire, or the Sunday school teacher will move to another city, but you, as long as you have breath, will be there. Will you be a lonely old man who has never generated the trust necessary to draw question-bearing children to himself, or will you be perceived as a sage, one who displays vigorous reasoning and dispenses proven answers?

Your role in maintaining the path upon which your children tread is up to you. Will they depart from it? Not if they've been trained and adequately supplied with a well-stocked shelf of defenses against challenges to the truth. If any of my children leave God's road, I will confess that there must have been something deficient in his or her training. Perhaps I was lacking as a father. Maybe my children refused their training regimen and rejected the path I set before them. I would rather search for an error on my part than assume that the Scriptures must somehow be wrong, that the proverb was incorrect when it said they would not depart from the right path. Let God be found true and His words remain trustworthy so that every generation may find hope in their promises.

## ✦ The Peripatetic Teacher

> And many peoples will come and say, "Come, let us go up to the
>     mountain of the Lord,
> To the house of the God of Jacob;
> That He may teach us concerning His ways,
> And that we may walk in His paths." (Isa. 2:3)

Although there is room for the role of professionals in the education of our children, they should be seen as adjuncts, helpers in our pursuit of teaching our children. We fathers are the primary teachers, guiding our children through the learning experience, building first a foundation of spiritual truth, and then delegating when necessary the other building blocks, whether they consist of academics, sports, or further religious study. If we entrust to others the responsibility to instruct our charges, we should review the material they're teaching. We should interact with our children to ensure completion of their studies and prevent corruption by influences we can't control.

Homeschooling provides a distinct advantage in our role as primary teacher. Although not all families can teach at home, many give up on the possibility without good reason. With education blossoming at home, a father can oversee all of a child's teaching, perhaps delegating the actual daily lessons to his wife or a multi-family group, sending to a professional for specialized lessons, or employing a tutor when necessary. The bottom line is that a father can watch over every aspect of his child's education, hiring assistants as he sees fit and monitoring his child's progress on a day-to-day basis. Homeschooling is the ultimate expression of a father's teaching role.

Even if homeschooling is impossible, a father can still create the bedrock upon which others will build. Since the most important part of a child's education is his biblical instruction, fathers should be in charge of that crucial element and not pass it along to another teacher. This responsibility includes not only daily devotions; it involves life instruction. Just as Jesus taught His disciples as they walked along, so should a father be ready at all times, looking for opportunities to instruct as he interacts with all of life's circumstances.

Jesus was a peripatetic teacher. Peripatetic literally refers to "one who walks around." As you "walk around" in your daily life, take note of the news you hear and observe the ways of people you see. Verbalize your observations to your children. When rumors of war blare from the radio, tell of past wars and how God worked them out for good. When you see the night scene on the streets, talk about how sad it is that some women dress so alluringly, thinking that exposing their flesh will attract a man worth attracting. Remind them of how Jesus had compassion on a weeping harlot and how we should pray for those trapped in the clutches of sin.

The opportunities for teaching through the daily expressions of life are practically limitless. They allow you to train your children to see their world through spiritual eyes and to discern the tragedy of sin in the world. By your peripatetic teaching, you'll prepare them for their solo encounters with the world and its corrupting influences, and you'll instill in them compassion for people whose hearts are far from God.

As valuable as this "walking around" teaching is, it is not a replacement for "sitting down" instruction. Daily Bible teaching is the foremost method of laying our educational foundation. If our children are not thoroughly grounded in Scripture, they'll flounder in the darkness when temptations and challenges to their faith arise. There's nothing more empowering or more stabilizing than being able to recall or refer to Scripture and speak the words, "Thus sayeth the Lord." The Word of God can be their sword as they fend off an enemy attack, but it will rust in its scabbard without regular use.

In our family, we begin each morning by reading a chapter from the Old Testament, moving through each book as the months go on. Each child reads a portion aloud, and when we're finished, we discuss any questions or comments. In the evening we do the same with a New Testament chapter. My job is to assimilate the information, simplifying the text for younger minds with a brief summary. Sometimes there's little or no discussion, especially in the chapters that contain nothing but numbers or genealogies. At other times, however, the discussion can be deep and complex, raising both doctrinal and practical issues. If there's no feedback, I'll frequently raise a question myself in order to pique interest and rouse the morning sleepyheads.

These interactions are informal, conducted without undue coercion or sternness. The lessons are also age appropriate. For our younger children, we read from a picture Bible, filling in important details that the simplified story might leave out. The drawings help the words come to life for younger minds, and they lay a foundation for the future, training them to hear spiritual truth. For our older children, I sometimes prepare a set of questions for them to ponder, even difficult ones that may puzzle them for a while. The goal is to encourage them to meditate on God's Word, to shape their minds into God-centered thinking machines. That way, when they're walking the path of righteousness, they'll be able to wield sharp swords to slice through the sinister schemes of the devil (see Eph. 6:16, 17).

## ✧ Preparation

Perhaps you're convinced that fathers are the primary teachers of their children. Yet you may feel inadequate, trembling at the thought of facing a question that seems to have no answer. A young child might ask, "Daddy, why are those babies starving in India?" or "Daddy, why do people fight in wars?" Your college student might open his philosophy book and ask what amounts to the same question, "If God is good, why is there evil in the world? How can He allow such suffering?"

How do we prepare for our role as teacher? Whether in the position of Bible teacher or question answerer, how do we obtain the knowledge and spiritual acuity to handle this monumental responsibility? First, we must learn to study the Bible for ourselves. We cannot rely on listening to a Sunday sermon, either from the pulpit or a cassette player. Another man's opinion may be helpful, but that's all it is, another man's opinion. If you have the Spirit of God dwelling within you, you have the ability to understand the Bible and discern its true meaning.

> But their minds were hardened; for until this very day at the reading of the old covenant the same veil remains unlifted, because it is removed in Christ. But to this day whenever Moses is read, a veil lies over their heart; but whenever a man turns to the Lord, the veil is taken away. (2 Cor. 3:14–16)

> But the Helper, the Holy Spirit, whom the Father will send in My name, He will teach you all things, and bring to your remembrance all that I said to you. . . . But when He, the Spirit of truth, comes, He will guide you into all the truth; for He will not speak on His own initiative, but whatever He hears, He will speak; and He will disclose to you what is to come. (John 14:26, 16:13)

There is no substitute for sitting down and reading the Bible, carefully pondering the words and prayerfully discerning their meaning, both the theoretical substance and the practical applications. It's also helpful to read apologetic classics such as *Evidence That Demands a Verdict* by Josh McDowell or *Scaling the Secular City* by J. P. Moreland. Don't be afraid to challenge your mind by adding secular philosophy to your reading list. Engage in mental battle with the authors so you'll be prepared to equip your children with the armor you develop during the struggle. Engage in conversation with older spiritual men in whom you trust, wise elders who have proven themselves through experience and holy conduct. Even if you disagree with them, ask questions respectfully, with the grace and innocence you would hope your children would exercise when approaching you.

And don't be afraid to change your mind. An uneducated mind is ignorant. An unteachable mind is arrogant. If a good set of arguments proves your opinion wrong, be brave enough to admit it. Only then will you be on a true course of learning rather than on a mission to prove a pet doctrine. It's also dangerous to accept a teaching simply because it's popular. A doctrine is not correct just because everyone believes it. A search for God's truth is more typically a lonely one, for few venture it with whole-hearted devotion, and even fewer are able to withstand the attacks of the mainstream.

When in class discussion, my favorite teacher, Mr. Burns, would ask questions to his students, each in turn, questions usually designed with a student's individual ability in mind. Although the tougher questions landed on the more capable pupils, everyone was able to listen to and glean from all the questions and answers. Once in a while, Mr. Burns would ask a question and get the "correct" answer, or at least what our book would say was the correct answer, and he would retort, "The book is wrong." The first time I heard him say that, it sounded like some kind of heresy. How could the book be wrong? No one had ever questioned any textbook's authority before! Mr. Burns would go on to explain not only the right answer but also how the book arrived at its inaccuracy, citing personal experience from his years as an engineer. I was more than impressed. This teacher had the intellectual courage to challenge the experts while carrying the academic authority to prove his challenge.

Fathers, as we prepare our children to fight against the schemes of evil principalities, we'll do them a great service by teaching them to think independently, to ask difficult questions, to reject pat answers and popular notions that carry no solid reasoning. If we give them the courage to say, "The book is wrong," they will not be quick to believe their professors or their peers, should those influences strive to steer them from God's path.

And it came about that after three days they found Him in the temple, sitting in the midst of the teachers, both listening to them, and asking them questions. And all who heard Him were amazed at His understanding and His answers. (Luke 2:46, 47)

Woe to you, scribes and Pharisees, hypocrites! For you are like whitewashed tombs which on the outside appear beautiful, but inside they are full of dead men's bones and all uncleanness. Even so you too outwardly appear righteous to men, but inwardly you are full of hypocrisy and lawlessness. (Matt. 23:27, 28)

## ✧ On This Page

There will come a day when we'll no longer be there for our children. Though treasured at their first hearing, our words will fade like dying echoes in the valley as time melts memories in its vast expanse. To keep our words whispering in young ears for multiple generations, we can write a journal of our beliefs, so that when we pass into eternity, there will be a lasting reference for our children to see, a paper and ink collection of our thoughts, our love, and our inspiration.

Since I'm a writer, I have ample opportunity to create a treasure cache of written words. I give my early drafts to my children to read, allowing them to ask questions and make comments while my latest book is being constructed. The feedback is not only practical for my book's sake; it is also invaluable in communicating my thoughts to my students, my progeny. When the book is complete, they'll have a written legacy to reference and to pass on to their children as well.

Very few have the chance to make their writings their profession, but anyone can keep a journal. Simple diary entries can relate your thoughts, hopes, and dreams, your concerns for the times, your prayers for the future. Don't discount the value of a well-placed prayer, a written pronouncement of your inner groanings. Even these can be a legacy as new generations witness your faith from the vantage point of the future, years after your prayer of faith stood as your saving shield.

## Faith's Journey

There is a path
That goes I know not where
Though savage beasts may prowl its edge
I trust the one who laid it there

What is faith?
A path unknown
Whose builder's name
Is signed in stone

There is a road
A course without a bend
Though blinded in the storms of night
I run as one who knows its end

What is faith?
A road so straight
That never turns
From heaven's gate

There is a way
A light of truth and life
Though wrapped in humble cloths of flesh
He breaks the chains of sin and strife

What is faith?
A way to see
Who lights the world
And sets us free

There is a journey
Of nails and thorns in flesh
Though blood and tears obscure the way
They purify the martyr's steps

What is faith?
The journey home
Is veiled in tears
Yet fully known

—BRYAN DAVIS

## ✧ Summary

Only give heed to yourself and keep your soul diligently, lest you forget the things which your eyes have seen, and lest they depart from your heart all the days of your life; but make them known to your sons and your grandsons. Remember the day you stood before the Lord your God at Horeb, when the Lord said to me, "Assemble the people to Me, that I may let them hear My words so they may learn to fear Me all the days they live on the earth, and that they may teach their children." (Deut. 4:9, 10)

In order to teach our children properly, we have to capture their hearts as well as their minds. We need to blend academic pursuits with the reasons they even exist to be explored—God's creative hand. Every observable phenomenon exists because God created it, so as we learn, we discover God's attributes.

Fathers instill trust in their children so they'll feel free to ask questions, even after they leave home and face the temptations of the world. We do this by our openness to difficult questions and our ability to answer satisfactorily.

Successful fathers realize that they are the overseers of their children's education. They don't give up that role to professionals who cannot intimately know the hearts of their students. They teach from life, being peripatetic in their practical approach to education, while also applying "sitting down" learning.

Preparation is the key to all these points. A father studies to be ready to teach and answer the questions that are bound to come up. Reading the Bible is the ultimate exercise, but studying and gleaning the works of others is helpful as well.

The final stroke of the father's teaching legacy is what he leaves behind in written form. His thoughts and dreams can last as long as the paper holds the ink, and even longer if a great-grandchild sees fit to copy it for safekeeping.

# The Father as Truth Teller

### ✧ The Truth Detector

We've all heard about polygraphs, the so-called lie detectors that, when connected by sensors to a person's body, read the subject's heart rate, respiration, and body movements. Supposedly, certain increases in activity alert the polygrapher that the subject is lying or at least being deceptive with his answers. Are these devices accurate? Though polygraphs have frequently been used to implicate or exonerate suspects during a criminal investigation, their reports are still not accepted as evidence in court since it's possible to fool the machine.

God, on the other hand, is never fooled. He has been in the lie-detecting business ever since He created man, and His ruling is infallible. Actually, God should be called a truth detector, for His very presence demands the truth, drawing confession from those whom He questions. Few are so bold that they can lie in the light of God's glory.

> And they heard the sound of the Lord God walking in the garden in the cool of the day, and the man and his wife hid themselves from the presence of the Lord God among the trees of the garden. Then the Lord God called to the man, and said to him, "Where are you?" And he said, "I heard the sound of Thee in the garden, and I was afraid because I was naked; so I hid myself." And He said, "Who told you that you were naked? Have you eaten from the tree of which I commanded you not to eat?" And the man said, "The woman whom Thou gavest to be with me, she gave me from the tree, and I ate." Then the Lord God said to the woman, "What is this you have done?" And the woman said, "The serpent deceived me, and I ate." (Gen. 3:8–13)

In the blazing presence of God's holiness, the first couple could not hide their sin. Light reveals truth, leaving no dark corner or murky shadow once it's allowed to shine. Light and truth go hand in hand with such inseparable attachment they're sometimes used as virtual synonyms.

> In Him was life, and the life was the light of men. And the light shines in the darkness, and the darkness did not comprehend it.... There was the true light which, coming into the world, enlightens every man. (John 1:4, 5, 9)

Since light brings truth, people who are of the truth bask in the light while those who practice evil hide in dark shadows.

And this is the judgment, that the light is come into the world, and men loved the darkness rather than the light; for their deeds were evil. For everyone who does evil hates the light, and does not come to the light, lest his deeds should be exposed. But he who practices the truth comes to the light, that his deeds may be manifested as having been wrought in God. (John 3:19–21)

As fathers, we are responsible for living out God's truth-telling character, modeling his trustworthiness for our children. As Jesus said, "While I am in the world, I am the light of the world" (John 9:5). Now that Jesus has ascended into heaven, we are His lights in this present darkness.

So how do we shine that light? How do we live the truth and detect its presence, showing the difference between truth and error, good and evil? Let's explore how we dads can be extraordinary lights, supernovas on the world's dark canopy. As we live the truth we'll be able to detect it in all of life's challenges and teach our children discernment, planting little lights in their vulnerable souls.

## ✧ Can You Handle the Truth?

Be diligent to present yourself approved to God as a workman who does not need to be ashamed, handling accurately the word of truth. (2 Tim. 2:15)

First and foremost, we fathers must be found trustworthy. As the Bible says, "Many a man proclaims his own loyalty, but who can find a trustworthy man? A righteous man who walks in his integrity— how blessed are his sons after him" (Prov. 20:6, 7).

We see many examples in this world of men who would rather lie than tell the truth. When circumstances become difficult, it may seem easier to deceive in order to escape a dilemma. In the world of unfaithful men a husband may lie to his wife in order to cover up an illicit sexual affair or to keep his late-night poker game a secret. Situation comedies on television are filled with men who deceive their wives. These men are fools who never learn from their bumbling attempts to tell lie after lie as their plots unravel. Politicians seem to lie on a daily basis, especially during election campaigns as they make impossible promises and smear their opponents with half-truths and innuendos. Cheating on taxes seems as common as bugs in a bayou as men use deception to gain whatever financial advantage they can.

Simply put, a man of integrity is rare, and the world is not accustomed to the light he shines. Though we often see lies and deceitfulness working to give momentary advantage to people who wield those evil weapons, we must not follow the world's model. Whether we enjoy gain or suffer loss in our quest to maintain integrity, we must never look at temporary results.[2]

You may hear people say they long for an honest man, but, in reality, practically the opposite is true. In fact, the most honest men in history have been ostracized, jailed, or even killed for not living according to the common deceptions of the day. Jeremiah was cast into a cistern for warning of a Babylonian invasion, John the Baptist was imprisoned and beheaded for daring to declare Herod's marriage unlawful, and Jesus was crucified for, among other reasons, exposing the hypocrisy of the religious leaders of the day. Shining the light of truth in a world of darkness carries great risks, and people who would rather hold to deception and hide in the darkness will attack those who shine the light, those who expose sin in secret places.

---

[2] I admit that there may be exceptions to this rule. In the Bible we see midwives blessed by God after they misinformed Pharaoh about the Hebrew women, and Rahab is commended for not telling the truth about the spies she hid on her roof. Whether or not lying is acceptable when trying to save a life is beyond the scope of this book. Here we are focusing on the selfish lie, one in which the liar is trying to secure gain or prevent personal suffering. Perhaps this is the very definition of lying anyway.

The questions for us dads are: Can we handle the truth? Are we ready to wield truth like a sword, bearing its burden of responsibility, willing to suffer the wrath of those who ruthlessly object? Are we ready to speak the truth in love, applying it like a healing balm to ravaged, searching souls? Consider carefully. The truth hurts. The truth also heals. It cuts both like a warrior's sword and a surgeon's scalpel. It burns like caustic acid, yet it soothes the one who longs for its cleansing power.

To earn the right to wield truth, we must first be willing to live the truth. Every category of life carries the opportunity to make a choice between the truth and a lie, between honesty and deceit, both in what we say and how we live. Our children watch our actions, which speak, as the cliché bearers rightfully say, louder than our words. If our lives reflect compromise with the truth, our children will have no reason to trust us—neither our rules nor our principles nor our exhortations to embrace faith in Jesus Christ.

Test yourselves. Do you speak and act the same way inside your home as you do on the outside? In other words, are you the same man in your sweat clothes as you are in your Sunday best? If you say spending time with your children is important, do you actually spend that time? After exhorting your children to obey the law, do you keep the speed limit and pay all your legal tax obligations? When you watch your children engage in sports activities, do you preach tolerance, fair play, and good attitudes? What's your own attitude when you're in the midst of intense competition?

Integrity is lived out in everyday circumstances, and loving, even adoring, eyes watch every move we make. When our children are young, if they see us acting in a way that doesn't reflect what we have taught them, their conclusions may not be judgmental at all; they'll simply assume that our duplicity is normal, and they'll mimic our behavior. Older children, however, may harbor resentment or even lash out, knowing that hypocrisy lurks in their home, personified in the man they have trusted for so many years. How can we expect

our children to live lives of integrity if we fail to show them a consistent model, a life that lives the truth even when the cost is high?

When I sold my shares in a privately held investment firm, I
realized a substantial gain. Of course, the government demanded a
percentage, so the members of our former partnership, who also
sold their shares, held a meeting and decided to declare an increased
cost basis for our stock, thereby reducing the gain and their taxable
income. The justification for the cost increase was spurious, and I
couldn't go along even though reporting the truth cost me several
thousand dollars in taxes. Though the federal government probably
would never have discovered the truth had I lied, I followed the
command of Christ and rendered a factual calculation unto Caesar.

My children would never have known about my decision either
way. Our financial dealings are a mystery to them. Dad goes somewhere, stays awhile doing some kind of barely understandable work,
and brings back a paycheck to buy food and clothes for everyone. I
decided, maybe because I wanted some good to come out of the pain
I felt in my wallet, to explain what I did and why. If I remember cor-
rectly, two of my seven children objected, claiming that the government
has no right to take our hard-earned money in the first place, but that's
the subject of another book entirely. We all agreed, however, that telling
the truth, especially when it costs us dearly, is a sign of godly integrity.

This episode, along with many others, has enabled me to stand
as a man of integrity in the sight of my children. And their perception is accurate, for I am a man of integrity.

Really? Is it possible to have such an elevated view of myself
while remaining humble? Yes, indeed. A father accepts this pedestal
as part of his job. First of all, a man cannot have integrity and then
deny that he possesses it. Such a claim would be illogical. Second,
we have to be worthy of trust and be willing to wear the mantle of
the household prophet, a new-covenant Elijah in our homes. Our
children need us to be bold, confident mouthpieces for God's Word.
If we were to shy away from this responsibility, we would be shed-

ding one of God's ordained battle vestments, the waist belt of truth. Unless we wear it boldly like a warrior, we'll shrink in shame when the flaming missiles fly.

> Stand firm therefore, having girded your loins with truth, and having put on the breastplate of righteousness, and having shod your feet with the preparation of the gospel of peace; in addition to all, taking up the shield of faith with which you will be able to extinguish all the flaming missiles of the evil one. (Eph. 6:14–16)

Christ's disciples looked to Him as the undeniable source of truth. Their doubts came only when they didn't understand the mysteries He purposefully built into His parables and prophecies. We fathers stand in the same place, teaching our disciples from a position of unassailable authority. If we allow even one shadowy story to escape our lips, if we permit even a hint of hypocrisy in our actions, we risk blowing up our prophetic pedestal, and perhaps nothing we say will ever be able to repair it, though we try to make amends through many tears.

Several years ago I agreed to coach my son's baseball team, though I had little experience with coaching and no understanding of the politics in the local baseball league. While going through the player draft process, I was warned by certain parents not to draft their children or they wouldn't play. I had to skip over "protected" players who had been predrafted by championship contenders, and I experienced other activities that guaranteed one or two stacked teams. I learned quickly that the playing field would not be level and that I had wandered like an unprotected lamb into the realm of ravenous wolves. I also brought to my team the philosophy that everyone should play an equal amount of time, hoping the less skilled players would learn from experience.

Our sadly losing ways brought us a perfect zero wins and nine losses halfway through the season, and the objections of some parents became louder and increasingly vulgar, even in public. I asked the father of one of our best players if he would take over the coaching position, and he agreed. I thought this move best for the team, replacing myself with a more experienced and capable coach. Unfortunately, I didn't foresee the effect this move would have on my son. I believe, though he wouldn't say so, that he saw my resignation as amounting to a lie, agreeing to do something and then not fulfilling my agreement. To this day I wonder if I made the right decision. I explained the situation to my son, made my apologies, and listened to his gracious words of acceptance. I pray that my place as his fatherly prophet was not permanently damaged.

Some may say that we should not even attempt to climb such a lofty perch, that we should admit our lack of integrity and give our advice from a lower level, communicating, as they might say, from one sinner to another. Such a philosophy is unbiblical and extremely dangerous. Jesus stood as the Light of the World and told us to be lights. Far from joining us in our darkness, Jesus brought blazing light to our lives and told us to spread it throughout the land. How can we spread his gospel without believing in our ability to be unfailing truth tellers? Paul told us he was an imitator of Christ and was unashamed to proclaim himself as one to be imitated as well. "Be imitators of me, just as I also am of Christ" (1 Cor. 11:1).

Those whom we are to imitate have gladly mounted the pedestal and have invited us to step up and join them on higher ground. They have girded their loins with truth and delivered it to the world without shame, knowing that truth comes from God as does their ability to preach it from the highest of mountaintops. They know in deepest humility that without God they are nothing, but they also affirm that, with God's help, they can do anything.

Any father who is satisfied with a lower standing, a platform that allows for the occasional lie, will find that his children don't trust him. Why should they? How can they know when his words are true? How can they know whether or not he has decided that telling a lie is easier than taking the high, harder road?

Since we stand in the place of the image of God the Father for our children, we must live trustworthy lives. If God were to lie on occasion, if He were to break a promise only once in a while, we could never trust Him, not for provision, not for protection, and certainly not for our salvation. We believe that God can raise us from the dead, destroying the ultimate fear in our lives. That's why perfect love casts out all fear, because we perfectly love and trust our heavenly Father to destroy the last enemy, death. If God were not perfectly trustworthy, we could never trust Him for a loaf of bread, much less to call out our names when we lie in cold tombs and to create for us resurrected bodies on that final day.

Fathers, if our children can't trust us, they won't feel bound to follow our precepts, our advice, or our faith. God in His mercy may guide them to the truth apart from our teaching should it be lacking, but there's no need to take that chance. It's also true that our children may depart from our words even if we've been good and faithful reflections of God's trustworthiness, but in those cases, they would wander off the path against all reason. They would be found fighting against their own minds, unable to shore up their excuses for not trusting our words. God can use our faithfulness, reminding our children of the integrity we held with unswaying passion, and draw them back to the way they should go (see Prov. 22:6).

## ✧ Of Storks and Santas

Being a truth teller begins as soon as a child's lovely eyes first cast their wide, wondrous gaze our way, as soon as her ears are able to thrill to the mesmerizing charm of our every word. In our children's youngest years, our words are golden. "Daddy says so" is the same to a child as "Thus sayeth the Lord," and all who hear such a pronouncement should lay down their shields, for Daddy has spoken.

Let's not give our fledglings any reason to doubt their faith in us. This may sound mundane and picky, but you shouldn't feed your children fairy tales and pretend they're true. Yes, Santa Claus, the Easter Bunny, and the Tooth Fairy may be entertaining folklore, but if you use them in celebrating special events, don't portray them as real. If you tell them Santa Claus brings presents on Christmas, if they're young, they'll believe you, especially if a pile of beautifully gift-wrapped presents magically appears under a brightly lit tree. A quarter that materializes under the pillow in place of a lost tooth is good enough evidence for any wide-eyed five-year-old. The Tooth Fairy really does exist!

Alas! When they grow older, the truth comes out. Someone outside your home exposes the myth and uncovers the charade, and the shock of reality damages more than your credibility; it endangers their faith. Did you think that believing in Santa was innocent fun? When your children learn you deceived them, what will they think? What other stories are really lies? Is Jesus a made-up story? Does He really bring salvation to all who believe in Him? Does God really expect us to obey, or is all that a myth too?

We've heard the song so many times: "He sees you when you're sleeping. He knows when you're awake. He knows if you've been bad or good, so be good for goodness' sake." Santa, the omniscient gift bearer, sounds like a god, one who happens to enjoy lots of cookies and milk on Christmas Eve. With this god exposed as a lie in the eyes of our children, will they view other stories with suspicion? What other lies have they been told? Santa is supposedly an all-knowing provider of good gifts. So is God. Will belief in God suffer if we appear to be liars about what is unseen? The Book of Life resembles Santa's list of good little boys and girls, and heaven might as well be at the North Pole; they can't go there to see God anyway. Doesn't that sound like another myth?

The simple option is to tell the truth. If we avoid the traditional lies of our culture, we can also avoid the danger of losing our children's trust at such a crucial age. Actually, teaching our children countercultural truths has an added benefit. If we confide in them that Santa, the Easter Bunny, and the Tooth Fairy are not real, and that their peers are being taught myths, then they'll enjoy being "in the know." In other words, they'll feel the privilege of being trusted with a truth most other kids are not given. We can also teach them to show love to their friends who might believe the myths. Exposing the game before their friends' parents are ready to do so themselves is not an act of love. In fact, an attitude that says, "I know something you don't know," is frequently rooted in self-satisfied one-upmanship.

As they come to understand that we were right about childhood myths, they'll be better trained to seek and trust our input when more tempting traditions press in on them or when their peers pass alluring messages into their minds. When we teach our boys to be polite and compassionate in the face of their aggressive and rude acquaintances, they'll be ready to be gentlemen in an age of ogres. When we teach our girls to dress modestly and act demurely while their acquaintances dress and act like harlots, they'll be ready to delight in the mystery of feminine purity, protecting their bodies and minds for their future husbands. When we teach that fornication is to be avoided, against the influence of the sexually active majority and even against their own hormonal urges, they'll be ready to fight its attraction. Treating our children with respect, as those who can handle the truth, will pay great dividends in the future, training their young minds to trust our words and encouraging them through our demonstration of confidence in their discernment.

As time passes and our children grow, our responsibility remains the same. Early in her life a toddler may ask, "Where do babies come from?" Will we tell her about a fleet of storks carrying newborns around the world, or will we tell her about the grand miracle of God's handiwork in Mommy's womb in words appropriate for her age and maturity? The questions will never end, and our answers must remain faithful to the truth.

Eventually, a day will come when my beloved son will mop my dying brow and ask me about my faith as I face death, the final enemy, and when my trembling lips utter, "I know whom I have believed," he will believe my last words and gently shut my eyes to this parting world, knowing that his father has kept the faith.

The time to start telling the truth is now. Whether our children are young or old, it's never too early or too late to start earning that prophetic pedestal, telling the truth in confidence that God will give you the strength and courage to speak and act in integrity.

## ✧ Lesser Men

As mentioned earlier, the media tries to promote an image of fatherhood that is far below the standards God has set. I call these images "Lesser Men." I remember watching the antics of Fred Flintstone, the cartoon cave man, who frequently connived with his friend, Barney Rubble, to deceive their wives, Wilma and Betty. Whether they were judging a beauty contest or running a diner they had purchased, it seemed that they were always keeping secrets from their wives, deceiving or lying outright in order to complete their outrageous plans. Of course, their plots were always discovered, and their foolishness was exposed, but the very next week, they were at it again, tiptoeing through a new field of freshly cultivated lies.

And that was supposed to be entertainment for children! The so-called adult programs are often worse, portraying men as cheaters, thieves, fornicators, and adulterers who use lies and deception to cover their tracks. Although some programs allow for these evil acts to bring about appropriate, destructive ends, few, if any, portray a strong father who consistently tells the truth and lives by sound principles.

The entertainment industry has poured its contempt for father-hood into the mainstream, depicting the best of father figures as bumbling fools who say whatever is necessary to get what they want. We have to combat its poison, and the only antidote is to live the truth. When we live in strength and wisdom, we battle against the common mind-set that fathers are worthless buffoons who are determined to follow their selfish passions. And as we counter those models, we may find resistance, sometimes from men who seem to enjoy the art of deceiving women, and sometimes from women who want to keep men in bondage to their desires, mere slaves who bring home paychecks and provide brute protection when called upon.

We're better men than that. We've been given the honor of reflecting the trustworthiness of God in our lives and from our lips.

O sons of men, how long will my honor become a reproach?
How long will you love what is worthless and aim at deception?
But know that the Lord has set apart the godly man for Himself;
The Lord hears when I call to Him. (Ps. 4:2, 3)

But the worthless, every one of them will be thrust away like
    thorns,
Because they cannot be taken in hand;
But the man who touches them
Must be armed with iron and the shaft of a spear,
And they will be completely burned with fire in their place.
    (2 Sam. 23:6, 7)

In order to battle the image of "Lesser Men," we must reflect a profound and better image, the image of God Himself. As we live the truth and pass it on to our sons and daughters, we can build a legacy for future generations who will recognize the Fred Flintstones of the world as a disgrace, an aberration, not the true image of fatherhood and righteous living. May God help us as we strive to erase the lies and build true models that will stand up and be recognized as normal images of God's fatherhood.

## ✧ The Truth Shall Make You Free

I realize many fathers have already failed at being truth tellers. Some have told "white lies" to please others or played the Santa Claus game. Others have uttered the most profane of lies, both with their bodies and their words, committing adultery, breaking their solemn vows, and lying about their actions to hide their evil and their shame. If you have destroyed your prophetic pedestal, what can you do? How do you restore faith and confidence in your character?

Jesus said, "If you abide in My word, then you are truly disciples of Mine; and you shall know the truth, and the truth shall make you free" (John 8:31, 32).

Living a lie is the darkest of prisons; its chains bind a man to its deceiving words. Trying to hide a lie often leads to more lies and more chains, each heavy string of links intertwining with the others to twist and choke out the breath of life. Confessing to any of the connected falsehoods would lead to the whole web of chains dragging the liar away to condemnation, for his first awful lie would eventually be found out as the failing wall of deception crumbles to expose his darkest secrets. When challenged, the liar's only solution seems to be to tell another lie, to cast yet another chain around his eternally burdened neck.

It need not be so.

There were those who dwelt in darkness and in the shadow
    of death,
Prisoners in misery and chains,
Because they had rebelled against the words of God,
And spurned the counsel of the Most High.
Therefore He humbled their heart with labor;
They stumbled and there was none to help.

Then they cried out to the Lord in their trouble;
He saved them out of their distresses.
He brought them out of darkness and the shadow of death,
And broke their bands apart.
Let them give thanks to the Lord for His lovingkindness,
And for His wonders to the sons of men!
For He has shattered gates of bronze,
And cut bars of iron asunder. (Ps. 107:10–16)

Shake yourself from the dust, rise up,
O captive Jerusalem;
Loose yourself from the chains around your neck,
O captive daughter of Zion. (Isa. 52:2)

The truth shall make you free! What joyous liberty! Though hiding in the darkness seems the most natural course for avoiding the piercing, painful light of truth, coming humbly into the light, exposing your deepest sin and crying out to the Lord for forgiveness and reconciliation is the only way to break the shackles and escape the prison. Don't wait until you're caught in one of your lies. If you freely confess, the contriteness of your heart will more easily be seen. Someone who confesses only because his most recent lie hasn't worked is nothing more than a trapped rat. A truly repentant man falls on his knees, not because he's pushed there from without, but because his God-pierced heart has buckled his soul from within.

The way out is a simple path; performing it may bring agonizing pain. The trauma of lost trust may mean a broken relationship with the one whom you deceived, but contrite apologies and true repentance are your only hope for restoration. If the one whom you violated is willing to forgive, a life of walking in the light, free of the bonds of slavery, awaits.

## ✧ Nothing but the Truth

As fathers who are living in the light, we'll be truth detectors, accurately identifying truth in this world of darkness and able to recognize falsehoods though they're disguised as truth. When our lives are immersed in truth, when we're always speaking truth, and when we're disciplining our children in truth, we'll be able to recognize anything that threatens to counter our efforts. A doctor can recognize the slightest aberration in a heartbeat because he has listened to thousands of examples of normal rhythm over the years. A skilled pianist knows when a performer misstrikes a single key in a complicated concerto even though no one else in the audience is aware. A gemologist can spot a fake diamond though it sparkles with a brilliance that can fool almost anyone else. As skilled truth tellers, we fathers can have the same experience, able to detect the beautiful melody of truth and identify any falsehood in its off-key disharmony, though many others would let it pass, unaware that God's music has been misplayed.

Truth is not just a passion for exactitude; it is God's way to salvation and freedom from sin. While abiding in the words of Christ, we will be truly free, never enslaved to our passions and never desiring to conceal our hearts, for a heart set free is one that walks confidently in the light. And in this way we will be able to pass on our light, implanting it in the hearts of our children, giving them confidence to trust not only in us but also in God, the giver of the light we faithfully carry.

## ✧ Summary

The light of God's Word is a truth detector. It exposes the lie and reveals the truth. We fathers are to shine as beacons of light, always bearing the truth as we live without hypocrisy, walking according to the truths we speak. Although we may be persecuted for telling the truth, we are never to succumb to the many pressures the world brings.

We live in a world that thrives on misinformation from the bearers of falsehood, from religious leaders to politicians to businessmen. Many people in every walk of life seek to suppress the truth and deceive others in order to gain an edge in their particular enterprise. Whether it costs us money, reputation, or freedom, we're commanded to tell the truth.

Battling the common media mind set of idiotic, lying fathers is best undertaken by example. Much of society expects us to lie as a normal way of life. Supposedly, it's just a masculine way to fulfill our passions, sneaking around to get what we want. As we live the opposite image, we may come upon resistance from those who prefer the status quo. We must engage the battle for the minds of men and bring together men of integrity who will lead our culture out of the morass of false images of manhood.

Following the truth is the only way to be free. Many men have gone the way of worthless images, and they need to break the cycle of dishonesty, repudiating their lies and confessing their deceptions. Their self-imposed bonds can only be removed through exposing their falsehoods and allowing the painful process of reconciliation to begin. If a man is caught in a lie, it's much more difficult for the wounded victim to forgive, but if a man freely confesses, the offended party can more easily see true contriteness of heart.

As we live the truth, we'll be able to recognize it and reject errors that masquerade as truth. Our experienced minds will be able to discern the perfect melody and harmony of God's Word, putting aside the discord of conflicting keys, whether struck blatantly or out of ignorance.

# The Father as Judge

## ✧ The Judge's Chair

> For if we go on sinning willfully after receiving the knowledge of the truth, there no longer remains a sacrifice for sins, but a certain terrifying expectation of judgment, and the fury of a fire which will consume the adversaries.... It is a terrifying thing to fall into the hands of the living God. (Heb. 10:26, 27, 31)

Sometimes it seems that God's role as judge is terrifying, revealing a dark side of His character. Such a perch seems too precarious for regular dads to ascend and take for themselves. The judge's chair is an uncomfortable seat, and his gavel is a ponderous hammer. Who really wants to take such responsibility, grasping the reins of justice and meting out punishments and rewards? Yet without God's perfect justice, without His decision to punish the ungodly and reward the righteous, there would be no real salvation for humanity, indeed, no real holiness in God's character. In the same way, without a judging hand in our homes, our children will lack the guidance provided by the law of God, an indispensable tutor that leads them to Christ (see Gal. 3:24).

This is a difficult role to reflect, perhaps the most burdensome of God's fatherly duties. But shall we avoid it? If we do, if we underestimate the value of the law or ignore its application, we endanger our children's souls. The law teaches God's standard, gives us a vision of His holiness, and exposes the sin that must be cleansed in order for us to find salvation in Christ. Without that judge's chair, without that sentencing gavel, our children will never learn the standard, the holy life our Savior lived.

When we subject our children to temporal discipline, whether it's a spanking, a loss of privileges, or an extra work detail, we reflect the eternal. We demonstrate that there is a penalty for sin. As our children learn how to respond to us in this earthly training ground, they will see their own sin and their need for salvation; they will be able to better understand the Supreme Judge and His requirements. As we portray the heavenly Father's justice, we'll help them escape the ultimate penalty, the danger of an eternity without God.

Enforcing the law is a stepping-stone, a tutor that guides our children by God's holy standard toward the One who lived it, Jesus Christ. When the law's work is complete, we can joyfully move on to the glorious conclusion of our labors, the salvation of our children, as we'll see in the next chapter, "The Father as Savior."

How we exercise our role as judge differs from child to child. Perhaps one shows signs of saving faith, another stands in open rebellion, and a third floats somewhere in between as he tries to learn what faith in Christ is all about. Yet each one needs a father-judge. The faithless child falls under the judge's gavel, thus crushing his rebellious spirit and teaching him the penalty of sin. The faithful child holds tightly to the judge's wisdom, asking for arbitration in a disagreement with a sibling or for discernment in helping him come to a decision. The ambivalent child watches the judge's character, testing to see if his actions match the code of law etched in his stone tablets.

God's judgment focuses on rebellious souls, but His role transforms into that of guide and counselor when the rebellious ones hold out their empty hands to receive His saving grace. Since God is our model, our role should reflect His ways, changing as our children change. And as they grow in grace, we have the joy of stepping off that elevated bench to come alongside as guide and counselor in the covenant of grace. We'll cover these aspects of fatherhood in later chapters.

## ✦ The Judge's Courtroom

I remember watching Perry Mason on television when I was young. The talented defense attorney amazed me with his relentless pursuit of truth, his ability to unearth evidence buried in sands of deceit, like an archaeologist patiently brushing away layer after layer to find hidden artifacts. His efforts always produced a result that became increasingly predictable as the episodes concluded week after week. During the court trial, someone other than the defendant would eventually confess his guilt as his involvement in the crime was exposed.

As a father I've participated in my own courtroom dramas. I've sat in the judge's chair, listening to evidence, both authentic and contrived, while dealing with the question of innocence or guilt in my children. Sometimes finding the truth is easy, especially when children are unable to hide their involvement in a family "crime." Their facial features or body language often shout their own verdict. Sagging shoulders and downcast eyes reveal the burden of guilt weighing heavily on their minds, while bright eyes and innocent smiles verify the unfettered joy of a blameless heart.

There are times, however, when a child can actively suppress the signs of his inner turmoil. He recognizes his guilt and learns to hide both the deed and his shame. The crime could be as simple as, "Who spilled the orange juice and didn't clean it up?" And every Bambi-eyed child in the house says, "Not me!" On the other hand, a father could stumble across a chilling, life-altering discovery, such as finding drugs or pornography in an obscure hiding place. Dilemmas like these would make me wish for Perry Mason to make an appearance, to stroll in wearing his tailored suit and wing-tipped shoes, ready to cross-examine the witnesses and eventually uncover the hidden culprit.

As fathers we are household judges. Although we have no formal training, no plaques on the wall reminding everyone of our advanced degrees from the great university of fatherhood, we dutifully climb into the judge's chair. Without a gavel, without a bailiff, we have the responsibility to hold court. Wearing a long, black robe might help. It could create an air of authority, but I think it would draw more giggles than respect. Yet, even without a visible symbol of our judicial mandate, we're called to divide between truth and error, to render impartial verdicts and deliver just punishments or rewards.

In Perry Mason's court battles, the judge had it easy. The brilliant attorney always managed to extract a confession from an unsuspecting witness, and his client invariably walked away a free man. With a pound of his gavel, the judge just said, "Case dismissed," and the newly revealed criminal was led to perdition, his head bowed and his hands cuffed.

I, on the other hand, have found that our in-house court dramas sometimes end with a roll of the dice rather than a strike of the gavel. I simply have no idea what to do. Black and white melt into gray as my children pour out an avalanche of explanations that justify their behavior, at least in their own eyes, and sometimes in mine if their stories make sense. When stories conflict, not only do I have to be the judge, I have to be both advocate and prosecutor, sometimes for more than one child at the same time.

At times like these I have to remind myself that being a judge is a fatherly calling, a role of my heavenly Father that I reflect. God is certainly One who expects us to give an account for our actions, and I model His judicial position for the sake of my children. Of course, I'm not the Supreme Judge. Since I can't know the hearts and minds of my children perfectly, I have neither the ability nor the desire to take that role. I'm more of a surrogate judge, disciplining with fairness and consistency to the best of my ability. As a surrogate judge, I receive my authority from on high and exercise it in humility, understanding my imperfect perception, but not shirking my responsibility even if I have to mediate disputes I would rather avoid.

For example, on an innocuous level, there's the ever-present "Who gets the toy?" feud. Upon hearing a cry from across the house, "He's mine! I had him first!" I know it's time to adjudicate another case, this one being submitted to the court docket as "The Case of Mr. Bunn, a stuffed rabbit." When I walk into the room, the child who's actually holding Mr. Bunn displays eyes of innocence, her smile proving that even a four-year-old understands the maxim "Possession is nine-tenths of the law." Her accuser, red faced and pointing a shaking finger, lays out the case for the prosecution. "She took Mr. Bunn from me. I had him first."

*Ah, the "I had him first claim." I've heard this before. Priority claim on a stuffed bunny is a powerful start for the prosecution's case.*

The defendant shakes her head and closes her eyes. "It doesn't matter. I got him for my birthday, so he's mine."

*The ownership defense in its purest form.*

"But it was sitting on the floor all morning. She can't expect to be able to grab it anytime someone picks it up."

*Score one for the prosecution. Casting aspersions on the owner's integrity.*

The debate can go on and on, and a father might be tempted to grab Mr. Bunn around his velveteen belly, making his blue button eyes bug out, and yell something like, "If you two can't get along, Mr. Bunn is going to do a belly flop from the roof of the Empire State Building!"

Would I ever actually say that? Well, maybe not. But I'll bet real judges are tempted to say far more than "Order in the court!" Our real response may require the wisdom of Solomon. What would he have done? I suppose offering to cut Mr. Bunn into two equal pieces might work, but our savvy kids have probably already heard about Solomon's strategy, and the attempt could backfire, as follows.

"I'll tell you what," I say, placing Mr. Bunn in a sitting position on the table. "I'll cut him in half and give each of you an equal share."

Their eyes light up. In unison they shout, "Cool!" And one child runs away calling, "I'll get the hack saw," while the other flattens Mr. Bunn on the table, his arms and legs spread out to await his untimely demise.

Such is the life of Judge Dad, the guy who now has to buy a new Mr. Bunn.

Seriously, this scenario is not far from reality. Difficult decisions face us on a daily basis, some having more eternal consequences than deciding Mr. Bunn's fate. And what if we make a bad decision? Will our children suffer because of our mistakes? Possibly, yes. But as we trust our Supreme Judge to correct our surrogate errors, we move on to the next case. Our fallibility is no excuse for avoiding our responsibility. Abdication of the judge's chair is not an option.

A career as family judge can begin with simple challenges, such as knowing when a child is lying. I'll never forget the feeling I had the first time my oldest son, James, lied to me. He was a month shy of one year old and already speaking in sentences, most of which made perfect sense. I don't even remember what he lied about, but the falsehood was a dagger that cut a deep wound in my heart. My son, the one whom I had nurtured and shown unconditional love, had actually lied to me! He chose deception to cover his actions, rejecting my love and authority. I was crushed. I felt a hint of the pain God must feel time after time when His image-bearing creatures rebel against Him.

In this case, judging guilt was easy; babies are poor liars. Yet delivering a just sentence, even in the presence of obvious wrong-doing, was difficult. I wanted his first lie to be his last. I wanted swift condemnation of the act but compassion for the child who had never lied before. I chose a stern voice, combining that with a firm, squeez-ing hand on his, while showing displeasure in my face and body lan-guage. "No!" I commanded, and then I repeated his lie, adding another firm, "No!" letting my scowl grow deeper and my grip tighten just hard enough to bring a twinge of pain. Yes, he cried. So did I. My grief over his first lie was one of the greatest I have endured as a father, and I knew then that more painful trials would come my way, other acts of turning from the right path that would tear my heart like wolves ripping flesh.

Children get older, and trials become more complex. Truth and error become more difficult to discern. Even if a child isn't lying directly, he may deceive his father with passive silence, even deceiv-ing himself with words of rationalization, excuses that conceal his guilt. His covering may be innocent, like Mother's skirts for an embarrassed toddler, but it could also be insidious, like veils that hide the brazen face of a harlot.

So how can we hope to find the truth or obtain a confession if our children can't or won't recognize their own guilt? How can we sift through conflicting evidence when those who provide it may not be able to see through hardened shells that cover their own hearts?

Though we've taken the first steps, to assume the judge's chair and hold court, we find that without supernatural help, our efforts to find the truth can only go so far. As each painful trial unfolds, we turn our eyes toward heaven and seek wisdom from above. There's no Perry Mason to force a confession, no Solomon to offer a dividing sword. Yet we have a helper, a guide who can aid us in probing the minds of our children, revealing the hidden thoughts and motivations of their hearts. God's Holy Spirit is our ally in the court. And His counsel is indispensable.

## ✧ The Judge's Counselor

The Holy Spirit reveals truth more efficiently than any flashy attorney ever will. He divides the heart of man with a sword sharper than Solomon's. He not only draws out confessions in transgressors, He guides the father-judge toward the truth, helping him see deeply into the hearts of his children.

Being able to receive our divine counselor's help comes at a price, the price of preparation. And this should come as no surprise. A courtroom judge must be qualified in legal disciplines in order to understand a case. If an attorney recites case law or uses obscure legalese, an unqualified judge would be clueless, unable to interpret the counselor's line of reasoning, thereby rendering his defense a total waste of time. A judge also needs experience in dealing with people. He must be able to command authority, identify empty rhetoric, and read body language, adhering to the law while empathizing with the contrite. He gains all these abilities through studious work and interpersonal practice.

Fathers, preparation is an essential part of our gavel-bearing position. As we learn to open our ears, our counselor, God's Holy Spirit, will speak to us. As we learn to recognize His voice, we will hear Him communicate wisdom and provide discernment, reminding us of the law's high standard and the need to offer forgiveness even as the gavel falls. He will cut through smoke screens and flimsy defenses and reveal secrets in the hearts of our children.

If a child harbors secret sin, it festers in his heart; its caustic toxins slowly burn his young soul. And he feels trapped. Evil influences whisper cruel lies, telling him to keep those secrets under cover.

Though he may cry out in his soul, the chains of sin stifle his voice; guilt and shame silence his call for help like an angry serpent tightening its squeeze around his heaving chest.

Who sees his toil? Who hears his muffled call? The Holy Spirit, God's searching presence, answers the feeblest call of the contrite. He is the investigator of souls, the revealer of secret sin. Once He wields His scalpel, no veil of flesh can hide a child's diseased heart, no bonds of guilt can resist the blade's sharp incisions.

As the Spirit brings forth verbal confessions, we can then do our part, guiding a child to his ultimate release in Christ. Here is where our position as judge begins to transform into that of an evangelist, a guide to salvation, and we have to be ready to deal with what may be a difficult reality; a child's willingness to harbor sin is a sign of spiritual slavery and a lack of saving faith. After all, what is the true test of a person's faith in God? It is his behavior behind closed doors, the character of his life when he is alone and only God can see him.

We have to be ready to face facts. A child trapped in sin needs more than discipline; he needs salvation. If he's involved in practices that tighten the chains of sin, without help he'll never find his way to freedom. He'll flail in a stormy sea, his head straining for a clean gulp of air while a dozen anvils pull his shackled legs downward, and he may not even know that each sinful choice adds yet another weight to his hated burden.

If we are prepared to listen, the Spirit's counsel is available to us, allowing us to probe our children's minds for areas of darkness that threaten to destroy their souls. The Spirit tests a wayward child's heart, bringing conviction and, we hope, repentance.

How do we prepare? By becoming intimately acquainted with God and with our children. Without a close relationship with God, we cannot discern the work of His Spirit as a counselor. We will not be familiar with His voice, the spiritual communication that comes from our God-altered minds (see Rom. 12:1). In addition, without a close relationship with our children, we cannot detect when they are troubled or when the chains of sin bind them, chains that keep them from worshiping God in spirit and in truth. In the next chapter I'll explain this dynamic more thoroughly, how a father can take that final step and follow the Spirit's guidance in leading his children to salvation and freedom from sin's chains.

Unlocking the chains of sin, therefore, requires two levels of communication. The first is spiritual intimacy with God, listening to His voice. The second is relational intimacy with our children, discerning their needful state should they be locked in Satan's chains. These two realms of awareness work together, enabling us to probe hearts and minds, to blend our own knowledge with what is revealed by God's supernatural, piercing sword. It is only then that our preparation to be a judge will be complete. It is only then that we can truly bring God's plan for justice and liberty into our homes. For God desires justice, but He yearns even more for liberty, our escape from the dominion of Satan and our refuge in His protective home. And true liberty is only realized when a heart is made pure and released from captivity to sin, when the Supreme Judge is able to see a new child in Christ and say with finality, "Not guilty!"

## ✧ The Judge's Character

How would you feel if you were convicted of a crime and then learned the judge was guilty of the same offense? Suppose, for example, you're in traffic court trying to get a speeding fine reduced, and you think you have a valid excuse. The judge, however, is unmerciful, demanding that you not only pay the entire fine but also the court costs. Disappointed, you walk to your car and drive out of the parking lot. Since it was his last case of the day, the judge leaves at the same time you do, and as you carefully drive the posted thirty-five miles per hour, you see the judge zoom past doing fifty.

Outraged? Yes, as you should be. And we see this kind of behavior in all walks of life and in all sorts of people, hypocrites demand-

ing adherence to a standard while they ignore the standard themselves. Politicians vote for laws they know they'll never obey. Pastors
and priests sermonize against their own unrepented sinfulness. We
rightfully groan in our hearts over such hypocrisy, and we question
how these people can have authority over us, ready to punish us for
the same crimes they themselves commit.

As fathers, the judges of our homes, we must not live by their
examples. If we allow even a shadow of hypocrisy in our lives, we
will make our role as judge completely void in the minds of our children. Trust will dissolve; our uplifted seat will plummet. We will
have no standing, for our two faces would speak in conflict, one
extolling the virtues of obedience and the other winking, telling our
children by our actions, "Don't listen to that other face over there."

Though we condemn the forked tongue of hypocrisy in authority figures, we seem to tolerate its insidious presence in most of
Christendom. In our current Christian culture, a popular mantra
sings, "We're all just sinners saved by grace." And the "sinner" label
gives to many a license to continue in sin, some taking their imagi-
nary permit to its logical end, assuming that any and all sin is
expected in Christians. "We're sinners," they say. "Therefore, we sin."

It's hard to imagine a more backward interpretation of the New
Covenant. It is true that we have all sinned and fall short of the glory
of God, but Jesus Christ came to change our lives. He has cleansed
us from all sin (see 1 John 1:7). He has provided power for obedience through God's indwelling Holy Spirit, giving us reason to consider ourselves saints and not sinners.

The "sinner" label can be applied accurately when speaking in
terms of our actions in the past, as Paul did when discussing his life
as a persecutor of the church, "It is a trustworthy statement,
deserving full acceptance, that Christ Jesus came into the world to
save sinners, among whom I am foremost of all" (1 Tim. 1:15). Yet,
when he spoke of his current life in Christ, far from calling himself a sinner, he said, "Be imitators of me, just as I also am of

Christ" (1 Cor. 11:1). In this second sense, in our current actions, we are not sinners. We are saints, actively doing God's will with obedient hearts.

The New Testament refers to Christians as saints more than sixty times. It never labels post-Pentecost believers as sinners, except when referring to their lives before they came to saving faith. This should be reason enough to take the label of saints for ourselves, not in pride of accomplishment or position, but rather in humility, knowing that God has done a great work in our hearts.

Because of this fact, that we are saints rather than sinners, we have no excuses. We cannot fall back on the popular myth of Christian sinfulness in order to justify bad behavior. The result of such a mindset not only disgraces the fair name of Christ, it destroys our standing as judges in our homes. If we're involved in sin and still pass judgment on a child, rendering a guilty verdict and handing out a punishment, why shouldn't he feel the same outrage we felt in the case of the speeding judge? Why should a child respect a set of rules when his father is unwilling to obey the rules that God sets?

But if we live in obedience, consistently calling on God for His power to live in holiness, our children will respect our position, knowing their judge will act honorably. As we give glory to God for forgiveness and cleansing, our children will understand that they, too, can access the amazing grace and sanctifying power provided by Christ. In this way, a just verdict followed by a reasonable punishment brings hope. It affirms God's holy standard, unveils the secrets of a heart under bondage, and demonstrates forgiveness, the compassion God felt for us in giving His Son to die in our place. And, most important, it provides hope for a better way—a redeemed heart and a new beginning.

If fathers cannot show that an obedient life is possible, children will have no hope that they will ever escape the clutches of sin. Disobedience, judgment, and punishment will develop into a cycle from which they will never escape. The popular, "We're just sinners" mantra will hold sway, and they will forever yield to temptation, believing there is no alternative.

We must model a different paradigm. Yes, the law is holy and must be obeyed. And, yes, violating that law brings about slavery to sin and due punishment. But there is a way of escape, permanent escape—the sanctifying power of God's Holy Spirit. And if we act as models of that sanctifying power, we will be the lights of the world Christ called us to be.

## ◇ The Judge's Code

How can a judge be impartial and just? Can he possibly render fair verdicts no matter how complicated the case? Since no human is omniscient, no father can possibly fully comprehend the inner workings of his children's minds, the motivations of their hearts, or the intent of their possibly misguided deeds. Sometimes children don't even understand these inner workings themselves; they can be bewildered by their own actions. As judges of children who might be living in turmoil, we must have a plan of action, a code of application that will help us render just decisions even when our children's minds are puzzles that seem to be missing a piece or two.

Justice requires consistency, a pattern of verdicts that cannot be assailed for their unpredictability or lack of a guiding standard. Justice requires refraining from showing favoritism for one child over another; it rejects excusing specific behavior one day and condemning it the next; and it refuses to bend the rules or overlook misdeeds simply to make the life of the judge easier. Holding to such a standard may seem hopeless, but if we strive for justice in the integrity of our hearts, even if we're proven wrong or found inconsistent, we can still command respect and honor from our children. Establishing a code of judicial conduct in the home can easily take up an entire book, but we'll go over some of the essentials briefly.

Being consistent is the hardest job I have as a father-judge. Not only do I have trouble telling the difference between a childhood indiscretion and true rebellion, I may not even remember how I punished another child for the same crime. And with differences in their ages, I don't know if the discipline I gave my twelve-year-old is appropriate for my eight-year-old who violates a similar rule. A younger child's understanding of our rules differs from that of the older sibling, both in maturity of mind and ability to carry them out. Why shouldn't the consequences of their transgressions be different?

The answer is simple: the consequences *should* be different. And our attempts to be consistent create this puzzling riddle: True consistency is sometimes born out of an appearance of inconsistency.

How is this possible? Consequences can be different for the same offense for different children, because, in a real sense, the transgression is different from child to child. Let's look, for example, at a situation in which a twelve-year-old does a sloppy job when taking her turn to do the dishes. After she's done, three plates still have caked-on food, and there's a milk stain at the bottom of two glasses. This child has proven her capability in the past, but today she was in a hurry or maybe even lazy. As a consequence, I tell her to do all the dishes at every meal for the next two days, hoping this discipline will remind her to fulfill her responsibilities.

But if my eight-year-old does the same thing, should she receive the same discipline? Maybe this was her first time dealing with dried spaghetti sauce or with such a big pile of plates. My decision is to take her through the process step-by-step to teach her how to handle a job she's never tackled before. My twelve-year-old cries "foul," claiming that I'm being easier on her sister than I was on her. What the older girl doesn't consider is that her sister has not committed the same crime; she was not hurrying, nor was she lazy. She was simply inexperienced.

Having more than one child guarantees conflicts like this. In their limited understanding, our children may genuinely not see the consistency of our actions, and that gives us an opportunity to explain that consistency is not achieved by a robotic response. In other words, Crime A does not always result in Punishment B. Consistency demands that consequences be based on our perception of the heart of a child and her maturity.

God handles two commissions of the same crime differently if the two sets of circumstances differ. In some cases, God's law metes out no punishment to someone who is ignorant, but it commands severe punishment when the perpetrator should have known better. (See Exodus 21:28, 29 for an example.) When we understand basic principles of justice and consistency, we can build a system of judicial application, a judge's code to live by.

The first and most basic principle of the judge's consistency code, therefore, is twofold. If your child transgresses the law in ignorance, handle it with a time of teaching. In contrast, if a child's transgression involves willful disobedience or defiant rebellion, hand down an appropriate punishment. Guide your judging actions using principles that examine the perpetrator's inner motivations as well as her knowledge of the rules and her ability to follow them. This way, you will have far more success in achieving true consistency than if you respond to rule breaking like a programmed robot.

A second principle involves your willingness to serve as judge even when you'd rather not. Times will come when it seems easier to look the other way when a child transgresses a rule. Or you might want to run away and hide from your responsibilities because of your grief over the sinfulness of an unruly child. You may be physically tired or emotionally weary of dealing with the same issue for the two hundredth time. You may be heartsick over the rebellious attitude of a precious son or daughter. Even then, you have to act in obedience, take the heavy gavel in your hands, and sit in the judgment seat God has placed in your home.

If you can't find the energy to deal with a problem immediately, it's better to delay judgment than to forego it altogether. Tell the child

you perceive a problem and that you'll deal with it at a more oppor-
tune time. This is allowable, for even God chooses to delay judgment
from time to time, but you must be sure to follow through on your
promise to deal with the issue. Idle words make a mockery of your
authority as a father. If you tell your children you're going to do
something and then fail to carry it out, you become something of a
babbler, a cartoon judge whose words are ignored.

Unfulfilled threats are popguns, frightening the first time they're
wielded, until the cork flies three inches from the barrel and dies in
a laughable, swinging pendulum. Broken promises are fake dia-
monds, sparkling and pretty when they're viewed riding on velvet
words. But when they fall to the ground unfulfilled, they shatter like
the transparent glass they really are. Both the promise and the
integrity of the one who made the promise disperse into stinging
shards, and the next glittering diamond is met with suspicion instead
of awe. After a while, both threats and promises are ignored as children just roll their eyes at Dad's silly words.

A third principle is to be patient, to investigate carefully to discover guilt or innocence. Avoid the temptation to jump to quick
judgment, because the truth of a matter may go beyond what you
see and hear at first. Get in the habit of questioning a child about his
motivations, asking him the reasons for his behavior. You may be surprised at how your child rationalizes his actions, and his reasoning
may give you insight into how his mind works. As he explains, you'll
learn his truth-telling tendencies and his perception of truth itself.
And he may surprise you. His passionate entreaty may convince you
to see things from his perspective, perhaps causing you to suspend
punishment, at least for the transgression in question.

This kind of investigation gives your children confidence that
you are actually pursuing truth and justice, not just trying to make a
peaceful home for yourself. You want to show them you're seeking
their hearts' compliance, not just strict adherence to a set of rules.
And searching their hearts with loving, probing words shows them

that you really want to know what's in there. Is it light, or are there conflicting shadows? Is there clarity or confusion?

Sure, sometimes a child will resist your probing. That's fine. There's no need to force the issue. Just tell your child in a gentle way that his reticence will oblige you to judge his actions based only on what you see and hear for yourself. Then carry out your judgment. At the very least he'll be aware of your pursuit of true justice. He'll see that a charge of unfairness will have no standing, since his unwillingness to cooperate with you forced your hand.

There will be times when your judgment fails. No matter how hard you try, infallibility in the skill of being a judge is beyond your reach. You may believe the wrong witness, see an act from the wrong angle, or misread a facial expression. An error in judgment can be extremely hurtful to a child, so be ready to admit your mistake should new information prove your decision wrong. An apology shows your children that you know you wear a fallible robe. By your admission, they learn that you're willing to listen to reason and are ready to change your mind should sensible entreaty be made. They learn to trust your heart-seeking ways, knowing that you desire what's best for them, the passionate, unshackled heart of a son or daughter, not the sin-fettered body of a slave.

## ✧ Summary

As fathers, we sit in the judge's seat; we're the arbiters of justice in our homes. Although we have no formal training or attorneys to help us find the truth, we're called to reflect God's desire to see justice done. He is the heavenly judge, the final authority, and we are His surrogate judges here on earth. Through us our children can see God's holy standard and experience the consequences of sin temporally so they won't have to experience them eternally.

We have a supernatural helper who'll help us find the truth in our trials. God's Holy Spirit probes the hearts of our children and guides our investigations. We have to be prepared, however, to learn God's way of revealing the truth. We have to know God and our children intimately, or we won't be able to interpret the symptoms of need or the signs of guilt. God will reveal sin to bring about justice, but God's greatest desire is to set prisoners free, to release them from bondage to sin.

As a judge, there's no substitute for good character. Judging those who transgress a standard while refusing to obey the standard ourselves is the height of hypocrisy. We must be in active obedience to God's commandments or we risk rebellion in children who'll see our inconsistency for what it is, pure hypocrisy. We are to be imitators of Christ, living as saints in this world of sinfulness. Living according to God's call will give our children hope that they, too, can escape the cycle of sin, that God has provided power for obedience. And because of our integrity, they will trust us, respecting our authority in the home.

Being inconsistent in our judicial decisions will damage our position of authority. It's important to adhere to a code of judicial application in order to render consistent verdicts. The first principle is to determine a child's knowledge of a transgressed law, deciding whether or not his misdeed came about through ignorance or was rather motivated by selfishness or rebellion. The second is always to be willing to assume our role as judge. We must never abdicate our authority by giving in to weariness, or compromise our integrity by uttering idle threats or empty promises. The third is to be patient, taking the time to discover the truth. Through diligent probing of the minds of our children, we may find an added benefit, a greater acquaintance with and a deeper understanding of their hearts.

# The Father as Savior

## ✧ The Light of the World

> Long my imprisoned spirit lay fast bound in sin and
> nature's night. Thine eye diffused a quick'ning ray: I
> woke—the dungeon flamed with light! My chains
> fell off, my heart was free, I rose, went forth, and fol-
> lowed Thee.                                   —CHARLES WESLEY

Darkness is more than the absence of light. It is a
prison. It binds a man by not allowing him to move in
the visual realm. He cannot be a citizen of the city of
light; he cannot even conceive of its presence, much less

its fellowship. A man in darkness, fast bound in the chains of sin, cowers if a flicker of light casts an illuminating beam on his poor, bent frame. Over the years he has learned to love darkness, its comforting familiarity allowing him to conceal himself from the blazing light of God's entreaty. He prefers its friendship. He takes comfort in the security of sin's chains. He is the Bible's Adam hiding from God's call, using leaves to cover his naked shame. He is Dickens' Manette returning to the labors of his bastillian cobbler's bench. He is Tolkien's Gollum in search of the Ring that binds him in darkness. He is every man, woman, or child who flees from the light, fearing its probing fingers and even shying away from its liberating power.

> And this is the judgment, that the light is come into the world, and men loved the darkness rather than the light; for their deeds were evil. For everyone who does evil hates the light, and does not come to the light, lest his deeds should be exposed. (John 3:19, 20)

One tragedy of sin is that the cure can be a foreboding remedy. Like a cauterizing iron, the light of truth pierces the soul, burning away the disease of lust, rebellion, and self-worship. The most needful of the cure prefer the comfort of their customary ways, avoiding the painful ordeal that opens the door to real freedom. God's light bearers know this terrible truth all too well as millions choose to close their ears and turn their backs when the gospel is spoken in their presence.

Fathers, our most important role in child rearing is to bring the Light of the World to our children, to be the glowing reflection of our Savior. Though some may hide from the light's revealing rays, we must be unwavering in carrying and passing on the flaming torch of God's revelation. We've already seen how fathers bring justice to their homes, making sure God's standard is upheld, that a clear delineation between light and darkness is always maintained. Without such a standard, our children won't be able to perceive the creeping darkness that grows along with their sin, the sin in which all participate before coming to the light.

In this chapter we'll see how to guide our children out of the land of enslaving darkness and into the city of emancipating light, how to combat the domain of darkness and its keeper, who seeks to keep them enslaved in his clutches, and how to shine the light so our own grace and mercy reflect those attributes of God our Father.

## ✧ The Light's Guidance

In the previous chapter we learned that God's Spirit guides us as we sit in the judge's chair, showing us how to reveal secret sin in our children. As we might expect, the same Spirit comes alongside us to lead them out of the darkness and into the light. These two activities of the Holy Spirit go hand in hand, for God doesn't reveal sin simply to condemn the sinner; He brings sin to the forefront in order to give a person an opportunity to change—to repent of sin and turn to God in humble submission.

Following the lead of your children's holy pursuer isn't an easy task, not one to be taken lightly. First of all, you need to be patient and not strike out on your own. Trying to hunt down and root out secret sin in a child when God hasn't completed His work is like trying to reap the harvest out of season. Only God can bring conviction, for only He can hear the hidden whispers of the mind and the inner groanings of a soul in bondage. Only He can know when that mind has cried out with Paul, "Wretched man that I am! Who will set me free from the body of this death?" (Rom. 7:24).

Second, you need to be aware of subtle nuances, tiny changes that help you detect problems, and take notice of opportunities to act. Knowing that God communicates using a still, small voice (see 1 Kings 19:12 KJV), you must be vigilant, always ready to listen for God's call to harvest. God can give that call in two ways, through your own observations and through spiritual perception. With your eyes and ears, take notice of the smallest alterations in your children's actions, their moods, or even their facial expressions that might indicate internal tremors or cries for help. With spiritual awareness, learn to listen for God's voice when He comes to you in a prompting gentle wind, letting you know it's time to take action.

How does this spiritual communication work? Every now and then I get a feeling that something is bothering one of my children. Whether it comes from knowing them so well or from a nudge from God's loving Spirit, I can't always be sure. On one occasion in particular there seemed to be a shadow in my son's countenance, a shift in his mood, a subtle turn in his expression that made me take notice. I felt God's Spirit telling me to check it out, because this latest turn wasn't an insignificant shift. Something was clearly wrong.

I asked him what was on his mind, inviting him to sit with me for a couple of minutes. He made an effort to gently shrug off my inquiry, giving an anatomical smile and an excuse for his altered demeanor, one he may have believed himself. He was not convincing. As I gazed into his eyes, I felt the Spirit of God come upon me, telling me exactly what was troubling my son. Somehow I was able to identify the darkness that painted his shadows. I questioned him about the subject directly, speaking with love and compassion, yet with a depth of power that made me tremble inside.

Being confronted directly with his sin struck him to the core. He turned red and began visibly shaking. He cried, nodding his head in confession, his face contorting in pain. As he confessed his sin, pure anguish poured forth, and in his agony he cried, "Please hit me!"

Oh, the grief that stabbed my soul! Clearly, this poor child had suffered for so long, and I was unaware! He begged to be punished, to suffer for his sin. He believed that pain would relieve his guilt, a bruise or a bloody nose to make amends for his iniquity. Yet, I knew it would not bring true healing. It would be a mere bandage for a heart that needed God's holy surgery. Someone had already suffered for his sin, had already shed His blood so my son would not have to bleed.

I grasped his shoulders and joined him in his sorrow. "No!" I cried, tears streaming from my own eyes. "It's not punishment you need. You need forgiveness and cleansing from sin." He wept on as I begged God to give me words of wisdom. Again I felt His Spirit touch my lips. "Don't you see?" I continued. "It's not so much the rules I want you to keep. I want your heart! Rules are good, but if your heart doesn't belong to God, rules make you a slave. God wants your heart first! God wants a son, not a slave."

The cooling refreshment of God's holy breath passed through the room, bringing its healing touch. I believe my son reached a turning point that night. Although I had taught these truths many times, he finally experienced the truth firsthand, feeling God's piercing sword and then His healing balm.

There is no doubt that my son experienced the depths of his own darkness, the painful squeeze of Satan's cruel cords of bondage. He felt judgment, the weight of the law condemning his soul, and he begged for release. In the torment of his imprisonment, he reached out for the only remedy that made sense, a buffeting blow of punishment, something, anything, that would give him the beating he knew he deserved. Maybe then the unreachable standard could be appeased. Maybe then he could find release from his chains.

But such a beating isn't what God demands for the contrite. The gospel of Jesus Christ doesn't scourge with a whip or clap a new lock on the chains of a slave; it freely offers redemption and the inheritance due a son. The prodigal son begged to be taken in as a lowly slave, but his father gave him a ring and a fatted calf, welcoming him home with open arms.

Our heavenly Father doesn't rejoice in punishment. He longs to distribute gifts of love, as Jesus said,

> Or what man is there among you, when his son shall ask him for a loaf, will give him a stone? Or if he shall ask for a fish, he will not give him a snake, will he? If you then, being evil, know how to give

> good gifts to your children, how much more shall your Father who
> is in heaven give what is good to those who ask Him! (Matt. 7:9–11)

It seems that when we ask God for a stone of judgment, He offers us the bread of life. Such is the nature of our loving Father in heaven. Such is our nature as earthly fathers if we imitate His providing hand of grace. Yes, we should be prepared to punish disobedience, but even more important, we must be ready to offer forgiveness, reflecting God's role as Savior to our repentant children.

## ✧ The Light's Illumination

From judgment of sin to realization of darkness, then from self-condemnation to repentance, we help our children on a step-by-step journey. When our children are able to perceive the darkness and turn to the light without cowering in fear, we need to carefully lead them to the final step of commitment to God by faith, using the guiding light we've already shown. God has searched their souls and found them wanting, and now it's time to show them how to loose the chains of slavery as we take them by the hand and lead them out of the wilderness of sin. It's time for us to shift from the role of judge to the role of savior.

Jesus said, "I am the light of the world," and He passed that light-bearing responsibility to us. We are now His lights in this world, as John wrote, "There was the true light which, coming into the world, enlightens every man" (John 1:9), and we have the wonderful obligation to shine, to be beacons for our children to follow. For them, we are the image of the Savior, Jesus Christ. Who better to guide them on their journey to the ultimate source of light?

And it can be a long journey. Some people surrender their lives to Christ in an instant, though for others the road to salvation seems an arduous passage, more of an expedition than a decision. Few people become aware of their inner darkness, their bondage to sin, and then immediately understand how to count the cost of following Christ and surrender all to Him.

This is especially true for children who've been brought up in Christian homes. All their lives they've been taught the gospel. They've been shown examples of obedience. They may see themselves as being in the light, especially when compared with people who care nothing about God and His ways. And maybe they don't harbor secret sins that cloud the thinking and darken the spirit of other young people.

In their minds the dividing line between light and darkness may not be clear. In comparison to their friends they may consider their lives as pleasing to God, and with society as their standard, they might allow themselves culturally acceptable sins. With the constant influence of their Christian parents and their church keeping them from the deepest pits of depravity, they may never perceive a need to shatter their darkness in order to come to the light.

In fact, our children could be in danger of being inoculated against the gospel, receiving the truth in a way that makes them resistant to perceiving their need. Like being vaccinated, their minds become immune to the gospel's life-altering flame. They feel like they're pretty good kids, bathing in the light of the gospel but not ever taking it into their hearts. They don't feel the darkness, so why should they feel a need for the light?

Many children of Christian parents are living their faith through their parents, assuming everything's fine because of the protective covering of a household of faith. They may not experience the more obvious ravages of sin that an unchurched child may suffer: drug addiction, pregnancy, rape, physical beatings, or sexually transmitted diseases. Such savage darkness may never attack their minds or bodies; they may never ache inside for release from torture.

These "Christian" children become so accustomed to seeing the light that it doesn't have the same effect on them as it does on someone who has known nothing but darkness. And when a child comes to the age when he needs to make his own choices, he may actually be blind to the blackness in his soul, seeing only the shades of gray to which he has become accustomed. He may have a sense that something's wrong, that he's not quite where he should be, but his relative goodness convinces him that everything must be fine.

This fact has been aptly illustrated in my own children. Though one of my sons and I had often met for spiritually illuminating discussions, he confided that his faith in God seemed academic, not personal. In other words, he believed in God intellectually, but he couldn't really connect with God in a spiritual way, a way that would change his life and free him from bondage to sin.

I asked him to examine his life when no one's watching, that is, when only God is watching. I told him if he allows sinful actions or thoughts in his private times, it would prove he doesn't really believe in God, at least not in the God of the Bible who takes account of every thought of every man. He agreed and asked me what he needed to do to have a faith like mine.

At first I drew a blank. Here was the time to turn on that blazing light of Christ and become a reflection of the Savior, and I was taken by surprise by my son's straightforward plea. I'm thankful God was ready to help, and I felt His Spirit once again energizing me. I started by explaining what my faith was like. I don't believe God exists simply because of various logical and philosophical arguments; I also know experientially that God exists. God is my ever-present counselor, the One who guides my steps as I put my feet forward in faith, the One who presents me with both blessings and trials as I walk according to His calling on my life. Although I wasn't sure at that point how to tell him the way to obtain that faith, I kept talking, knowing from experience that God would continue to speak through me. The words would come.

I told him that becoming immersed in the Bible was his first priority, that my own relationship with God began that way. I became obsessed with knowing God's Word. My attitude was, "If God said it, then I want to know what He said!" My heart sang with the psalmist, "As the deer pants for the water brooks, so my soul pants for Thee, O God." I became so filled with God's Word that I was able to mentally carry it with me wherever I went. Whether I'm driving or walking or waiting in line, God brings His Word to my mind, because I've made it so dear. Whatever the situation, whether celebration or crisis, God uses what I've learned by bringing the appropriate passage to the forefront of my thoughts.

I told him his second step should be to establish an emotional relationship with God that could blend with his intellectual understanding. God is a loving, gracious, compassionate heavenly Father who actively seeks out people who will worship Him in spirit and truth. Worship in spirit and truth means we are to approach God with our hearts and with our minds. A spiritual worship involves our hearts, allowing us to communicate with the heart of God, creating an emotional attachment between the Father and His beloved child. Worship in truth involves our minds, giving us a solid bedrock of understanding that undergirds our emotional attachment. In other words, if our emotions fail us because of a crisis that brings our happy moods crashing down, the impenetrable rock of God's truth keeps us standing firm. We remember the unfailing truth of God even if circumstances bring chaos and grief. Both aspects of fellowship with God are important, and once truth is established, we nurture an emotional attachment through personal times of prayer and worship.

The third step involves the most basic practical application of knowing and following Christ, being a servant. Jesus Christ came to earth as one who serves. From patiently teaching ignorant fishermen to washing the feet of His less-than-humble disciples, Jesus was a walking illustration of God's love. By giving ourselves in service to others, we learn the mind of Christ.

To know Jesus intellectually provides bedrock, a foundation to do His will. To know Him emotionally gives us energy and motivation to work, passion and drive to see a project to completion. To know Him experientially in the working out of His love actually builds His house. God's house is made up of those who follow Him in obedience, and the only way to bring people to His saving grace is to show them His loving character. Since we are Christ's representatives on the earth, the only way to accurately reflect His nature is to live out a servant attitude.

Such was God's helping hand in guiding my son. Even while I was speaking the second of the three steps, I didn't know what the third step would be, though I knew there would be one. God graciously used my mind and my words as His tools to guide my son closer to Christ.

My son is still in the midst of his journey, a path I trust will lead him to a deep abiding relationship with his Savior. His willingness to seek that relationship is the key, the first step on the road, and that should be enough for our gracious God to carry him the rest of the way. As his father, I will continue to monitor his progress, helping him avoid the journey's dangers. The light is now in front of him, and he gazes at it without fear. As long as he keeps his eyes fixed on the Savior, he will find the salvation he's seeking.

Our application, then, is to be ready to shine the light when the Spirit's work is complete, to guide our children to the next step on their journey, the step of salvation. We need to be aware of the shades of gray in their hearts, the "little sins" that arise from their lack of true personal faith. Though light has surrounded them, they may assume too much, that they are somehow automatically included as one of the citizens of light. The three steps I taught my son are essential parts of the Christian walk of faith. Let's make sure our children understand their need to wholeheartedly take that faith as their own, absorbing it as a self-sacrificing passion, not as a birthright.

## ✧ The Light's Spectrum

Along with being ready to speak the words of Christ to our children, we also have to show the saving grace of Christ in ourselves, our actions reflecting the compassion He displayed. Although Jesus had little mercy for the hypocrites of His day, He was always ready to offer mercy and forgiveness to the lowly and contrite. Although He is the ultimate judge, He is also the great emancipator, telling a woman caught in adultery, "Neither do I condemn you; go your way. From now on sin no more" (John 8:11).

The Light of the World displays a spectrum, a range of behaviors that shine through according to the need of the moment, according to the action necessary at a particular time. For the hypocritical scribes and Pharisees, Jesus showed no mercy, calling them blind guides of the blind. For the sinful woman who cleaned His feet with her hair and tears, He showed deep compassion while correcting those who criticized her. For His disciples He showed a blend of mercy and judgment, reaching out to save Peter from drowning yet reproving him even as they stood upon the waters, saying, "O you of little faith, why did you doubt?" (Matt. 14:31). In the same way, fathers, we need to be aware of how we shine the light in its various shades of judgment and mercy.

"What would Jesus do?" is not just a trite saying; it's a real question you should ask. For example, if you become frustrated with your children when they break the same rule over and over, what do you do? Jesus became frustrated with His disciples. "O unbelieving and perverted generation," he said, "how long shall I be with you? How long shall I put up with you?" (Matt. 17:17). Yet He never sent them away. He continued to teach and show forgiveness, living out His own instruction to forgive seventy times seven times. Fathers need to have the same attitude. After you administer the necessary discipline, and if your children demonstrate repentance, offer forgiveness over and over again. This is the grace end of the light spectrum, mercy for the contrite.

You should not, however, casually give out forgiveness when there is no hint of repentance. God our Father grants no forgiveness without brokenness of heart and change of mind in His disobedient creatures, so why should earthly fathers? If you were to offer restoration of fellowship without the necessary change of attitude in the perpetrator of a bad deed, you would be telling a lie about the nature of God. God will not allow into fellowship a person who is in active rebellion against Him.

Since you are to reflect God's fatherly attributes, you should keep a child out of your good graces if he harbors an attitude of sinful behavior. Offering forgiveness prematurely may actually endanger him. It tells him that forgiveness is available without self-examination and real repentance, a supposition that isn't true in the spiritual realm. Combat the idea that God will accept him just as he is, that is, in rebellion and without a desire to change. This is the judgment end of the spectrum, condemnation and isolation of a stubborn, wicked heart.

And as you might expect, your children will probably display many blends of contrition and stubbornness between the two extremes. Many children have divided hearts, demonstrating a willingness to do what's right yet finding it a hard chore because of the allure of the world's system and the desires of the flesh. As you use your light to lead them to salvation, condemn the evil act and offer forgiveness when God's Spirit brings conviction and repentance. In this way your light will shine with every part of the spectrum that God intended.

## ✧ The Light's Expanse

Every child must choose his own way. Born into a dark world and not yet acquainted with God's abiding fellowship, a child searches for security, perhaps groping for someone to love and someone to love him in return. This is the ache we all feel if we haven't yet found the light of Christ, if we haven't yet discovered the fellowship with God that comes through His indwelling Holy Spirit. There's a longing that never ceases, a pain that goes on and on, and if a child doesn't fill that longing with the presence of God, he will seek a

THE FATHER AS SAVIOR

replacement, a counterfeit light that promises the same benefits: power, friendship, and freedom.

A child may clearly see his darkness; he may feel the weight of his chains. And if somehow we fail to convince him that the light we bear promises the escape he desires, he will look for another way out. What do you do if a child turns completely away from the true Light and actively pursues darkness? He seems to care nothing for God's Word and has abandoned the principles you've taught. Or perhaps you got a late start in teaching the Word, and your children were already steeped in the ways of the world's system, and the light of the gospel is not attractive to them at all.

Take heart. The Light of the World reaches beyond the home. God is a pursuer of men's souls, and He searches with all the love and diligence we might expect from our creator. Jesus made this attribute of His Father clear.

> What man among you, if he has a hundred sheep and has lost one of them, does not leave the ninety-nine in the open pasture, and go after the one which is lost, until he finds it? And when he has found it, he lays it on his shoulders, rejoicing. And when he comes home, he calls together his friends and his neighbors, saying to them, "Rejoice with me, for I have found my sheep which was lost!" I tell you that in the same way, there will be more joy in heaven over one sinner who repents, than over ninety-nine righteous persons who need no repentance. (Luke 15:4–7)

Can you picture this in your mind? God, our heavenly Shepherd, takes His lantern and searches in the dark wilderness for a wayward child. At every moment, God knows where the child is, but as He approaches, calling out His precious one's name, His voice and His penetrating light have the same effect they had before, bringing to the child the same painful feeling of exposure, the same desire to hide in shame. The child may run away again, hoping either to find a place where God will not look or to corrupt himself to such an extent that in ashes of bitterness and self-desecration he mutters, "Maybe now God will leave me alone."

Such is the price and, sometimes, the tragedy of free will. A child may indeed choose to run from the blazing light of God's glory. Just as Adam did at the beginning, a child may flee God's call and pluck fig leaves to hide his shame, dressing himself in the camaraderie of this world. In other words, since "everyone else is doing it," he takes comfort in hiding in the crowds of those who share his sin.

This kind of hardening to God's grace seems irreversible. If a child has already heard the Word of God and rejected it, what more can he be told? And it seems sometimes that the more a Christian tries to retrieve a lost soul from this condition, the more hardened the rebellious one becomes. Still, the light we bear can extend even to the deepest den of sin the world can dig. As the psalmist wrote:

> Where can I go from Thy Spirit?
> Or where can I flee from Thy presence?
> If I ascend to heaven, Thou art there;
> If I make my bed in Sheol, behold, Thou art there. (Ps. 139:7, 8)

Who can know if a child's heart is fully hardened? Love calls us to have hope. Love calls us to take that lantern and search in the wilderness for our wayward son or daughter. Our search may seem hopeless, and our best efforts may come only through prayer. Even if all seems lost, we can ask God to rekindle the light He poured into our children, to remind them of our love and the truth they heard from His Holy Word.

Maybe God will use a dying ember of His radiance to cast shadows of doubt on the counterfeit light. Maybe the child's wayward path will finally come to a dark, hopeless dead end, and the only way out will be to turn back and once again behold the True Light that now casts those shadows. Maybe the false promises of the counterfeit light will break into pieces before his eyes as his so-called friends abandon him one by one.

Our light, living on in the word we implanted, extends beyond our physical boundaries. Its influence travels with our children. The prodigal son carried a light that finally opened his eyes. It enabled him to feel the aching hunger in his belly and hear the sounds of his only remaining friends—the slurping grunts of hungry pigs. And he knew even they would leave him if he were to stop feeding them.

No matter how brazen a child might appear on the outside, we can trust that God continues to work on the inside. A young man, penniless and stripped of his autonomous pride, weeps alone in a stark, dingy apartment. A young woman, her body used by a man full of promises and then cast aside in contempt, cries out in despair from her sin-stained bedroom. These children have come to the land of waste. What will be their end?

Our responsibility as fathers, while praying earnestly during those dark days, is to allow life to go on without our spiritually departed loved one. This demonstrates our faith in God's pursuit of souls and shows that the world does not revolve around a prodigal child. We cannot have normal fellowship with a rebellious soul. Pretending everything's fine doesn't reflect the truth about God's judgment of unrepentant sin. Restoration of fellowship without a change in the heart of the wayward child also brings poison into the home. It tells our other children that there are no serious consequences for sin.

Yet, our duty is also to be waiting with open arms when he or she returns, not to welcome an unrepentant rebel, but to joyfully lift up a child who utters words like these, "Father, I have sinned against heaven and in your sight; I am no longer worthy to be called your son" (Luke 15:21). There will be no hint of "I told you so," neither on our lips nor in our minds. We will celebrate, our minds shouting, "this son of mine was dead, and has come to life again; he was lost, and has been found" (Luke 15:24).

We implanted the light of Christ, it penetrated the souls of our children, and it remained embedded in their hearts, working to bring them to salvation or to rescue them from destruction. Fathers, we are the earthly reflection of God the Savior. In this duty we merely carry the light of another, but it is our most important calling, to shine forth with all the brilliance of one redeemed by that light. This is our ultimate goal—and all others pale—that our children can see Christ in us, the hope of glory (see Col. 1:27).

## ✧ Summary

Fathers, we act as the Light of the World for our children, guiding them through the darkness and toward the ultimate source of our light, Jesus Christ. Combining our awareness of our children's behavior patterns with our spiritual perception, we use the Holy Spirit's guidance to identify sin and loose its shackles. We take the time to show our deep abiding love, that we truly care for their welfare, both physically and spiritually. That way, when we talk with them, we may get the opportunity to explore the depths of their spiritual condition. We may learn that all is well, but we may instead find darkness. These are the times when we must be ready to guide them toward the light of salvation.

The journey toward salvation or toward maturity in Christ can be a hard road, even for children raised in Christian homes. Without a clear delineation between darkness and light in their lives, they might not perceive a need for salvation. Many of them haven't known the darkness of evil; they haven't felt the chains of sin. Their intellectual understanding of faith in Christ and their lifelong stand under the umbrella of parental devotion may have resulted in their spiritual inoculation.

Along with the intellectual foundation of truth, a child needs the emotional attachment to God that personal prayer and worship bring. He also needs to learn the mind of Christ experientially,

building the house of God through service, the practical outwork-
ing of real faith.

As fathers, we show all aspects of the saving Light of the World,
shining every color of the grace and judgment spectrum. We condemn unrepentant rebellion and offer forgiveness to the contrite,
always being ready to take a weeping child back into our good graces.
Each day can bring a blend of these two extremes, and the light we
bear can shine the proper hue according to the need of the moment.

Sometimes a child will completely reject the light, choosing the
darkness of sin and autonomy. In these cases, we go on with life,
constantly praying that God's light will be rekindled in the wayward
child's heart. On the one hand, we can make entreaty for his
return, opening our arms to the child who offers a heart of contrition. On the other hand, we cannot take an unrepentant son or
daughter back into our homes. Such an act tells the child a lie about
God's character, and it tells his siblings that we tacitly approve of
reprobate behavior.

# The Father as Guide

## ✧ The Journey's Next Step

> My son, observe the commandment of your father,
> And do not forsake the teaching of your mother;
> Bind them continually on your heart;
> Tie them around your neck.
> When you walk about, they will guide you;
> When you sleep, they will watch over you;
> And when you awake, they will talk to you.
> For the commandment is a lamp, and the teaching
>   is light;
> And reproofs for discipline are the way of life.
>   (Prov. 6:20–23)

A child is on a journey, a years-long journey of growth and maturing. Her stumbling, barefooted baby steps stretch into confident, patent-leather strides as she moves from speaking her first intelligible words to reciting a tenuous alphabet. Cloth picture books give way to chapter books, and tricycles are doffed in favor of bicycles. Each milestone is greeted with proud words and hugs from Daddy and a challenge to prepare for the next exciting step. Now she releases your finger from her tightly clutching fist as she takes her first wobbly ride down the sidewalk without her training wheels. You pace alongside, alternating between watching her widening eyes and rapturous smile and eyeing the thirty remaining feet of concrete between her and the corner.

*Steady, now,* you mentally prompt. With quick glances you survey her equipment from the top of her professionally fitted safety helmet down to her glow-in-the-dark kneepads and double-laced shoes. Every second of unaided pedaling is a victory; every crack in the sidewalk is the border of a new frontier. With a tear in your eye, you realize that this is an image of the future, another step toward maturity, to freedom, autonomy, life without needing Daddy.

That final step will come. Your son will exit your front threshold, one hand holding a diploma and the other waving with smiling optimism, the world of opportunity awaiting. Your daughter will waltz away in step with another man, the altar of marriage having embraced them in its covenant. Only then will your overarching protective hand fall back to your side, a change of life we'll discuss in chapter 12, "The Father as Counselor."

For now, the journey continues. While they're still in your home, your hedge of protection stays encircled, perhaps slowly widening as their boundaries of freedom expand. Even if your children have already taken the crucial spiritual steps through the wilderness of the law of God and into the promised land of salvation, their journey doesn't end there. Many tenuous steps remain. They need your guiding force throughout their young lives, watching over their decisions, directing their future steps, and providing shelter from the dangers the world may bring.

God our Father is surely a guide, leading us in times of peace and safety as well as in times of trouble. Again, He is our perfect model. He directed the Israelites with a pillar of fire; He led Joseph from slavery to lifesaving dominion; and He guided His only begotten Son from a humble manger to the ultimate sacrifice on the cross.

What can we learn from studying the legacy of God's guiding hand? What aspects of His leadership can we apply? If we look at the many examples of God's loving guidance in the Bible, these features abound: compassion, patience, direction, and purpose.

That fourth feature, purpose, is the next goal in our children's journey; it is their vision for the future. After receiving saving grace and the power to live for God, they will be called to serve in His kingdom. As we help them discover their purpose and lead them toward a vision, we will carry out our last great directive as fathers. But first we have to establish the groundwork for our fatherly guidance, the implanting of trust in their minds, trust that we have the wisdom and ability to help them seek and discover God's will. That trust will come as we foster the three preparatory qualities God displayed in His guiding ways: compassion, patience, and direction.

## ✧ Compassion—Empathy for Young Hearts

When children are young, their problems are often simple: dark closets, skinned knees, sibling rivalries, and maybe a vicious stray dog or a violent thunderstorm. Coming to you for help is an automatic response. Their first option for perceived danger is a cry for Daddy, and like a heroic knight you charge in and bring peace and safety to their world.

These early years give you opportunities to lay a foundation of compassion, a generous dose of empathy for your children. Do you remember what it was like to be small and afraid, vulnerable and alone? Can you put yourself in a child's place and imagine the monsters behind the shadows?

When God led the Israelites out of Egypt He took note of their fears.

> Now it came about when Pharaoh had let the people go, that God did not lead them by the way of the land of the Philistines, even though it was near; for God said, "Lest the people change their minds when they see war, and they return to Egypt." (Exod. 13:17)

God had compassion for the people because of their weaknesses; He understood their trembling ways. In like manner, a father shares an empathetic connection with his children. If you belittle their concerns as trivial, even though they seem minuscule, you will damage a precious trust. If you force them into situations they can't handle physically or emotionally, they won't believe that you understand their hearts and minds.

"Daddy, please shut the closet door."

After kissing his forehead you look at the open closet and walk toward it. "Why? Are you scared of something?"

He just stares at it for a second and then shakes his head quickly, tight-lipped and wide-eyed.

Although you smile on the inside, you maintain an air of serious concern and poke your head in the closet. Rustling through the clothes, you speak while you search. "Is anybody in here?" you call, loud enough for your son to hear. After enough time to thoroughly investigate, you come out. "I didn't see anything," you say as you pull the door closed, "but I'll shut it anyway."

Then you walk back to his bed and tuck him in securely. "When I was your age, I was scared of a lot of things, but God taught me that He's always watching over me. One of the psalms says, 'In peace

I will both lie down and sleep, for you alone, O Lord, make me live in safety.' When I learned that, I felt a lot better. I know He's watching over you, too, so you don't have to worry about anything while you're sleeping."

Connect with their fears, even if they're unfounded. Offer them reasons to dispel their fears, an investigation of the scary closet and a promise from the Word of God. Give them time to overcome their fears, hoping that God's Word will implant itself in their hearts as an empowering sword of courage. A bond of trust will develop as you demonstrate compassion while instilling strength.

As children move past their early years and their problems grow more complex, we hope they'll continue to seek us out for advice, regarding us as confidants and wise counselors. While we guide them forcefully in areas of morality and other biblical principles, when it comes to fears, education, friends, and careers, we step back a bit and try to influence their minds with whatever wisdom we have gained through our own experience. With each decision-making event, as we continue to incorporate a compassionate approach, we give our children every reason to believe that we empathize, that we consider their mountains to be more than the molehills they might seem to us. This way, they have no reason to worry about rejection or ridicule whether they ask about an open closet or, later, their choice of a spouse.

## ✧ Patience—The Gift of Waiting

As you guide your children, remember the vision. God's ultimate purpose should always be in the forefront of your mind, but it should not necessarily flavor every word of guidance you speak. In other words, although the vision is the goal, don't let its glory overwhelm a child's feeble steps beyond the plodding pace he can endure. Otherwise, the vision could become an object of resentment, a dreaded hammer that threatens to flatten him over every failure, rather than a joyous expectation of maturity or liberation.

"Son, you have to do your algebra. I know it's hard sometimes, but it's important."

He drops his pencil and looks imploringly at you. "Important? How can all these dumb old *x*'s and *y*'s be important? It's boring!"

A temptation rises to remind him of his vision, his desire to work at NASA to help launch rockets or even become an astronaut himself. Rocket science requires math skills far beyond his algebra lesson, so this stepping-stone is crucial. But you've used this tactic before. Reminding him of his NASA aspirations got him to do his homework the first two times, but the last time you tried it, he just sighed and rolled his eyes. His vision has become a hammer.

When God led the Israelites through the wilderness, he gave them symbols that represented their purpose, their entrance into the land of promise. He gave them manna, a pledge of daily provision. He gave them Sabbath rest, a reminder of a final place to rest from their labors. And He gave them the tabernacle, an ever-present tent of holiness that fed their spiritual longing, the desire to come into the abiding presence of God Himself, the ultimate Promised Land.

"Tell you what," you reply, taking his pencil and closing his book. "Take a break. Rest your brain from all those letters and come back to it later."

You drive to the mall and buy the most beautiful poster of a space shuttle launch you can find, and you come home and present it to him solemnly. "I found this, and it made me think of you." As he unrolls the tube of paper, his eyes light up. Without a word and without reference to algebra you have reignited the vision and given him a symbol that will strengthen his resolve. If God has truly implanted that vision, your son will probably return to those dumb ol' algebraic letters on his own. If he doesn't respond, you will have to find other means to get him to do his homework, something that will not raise his vision as a dreaded hammer.

The journey of childhood gives us plenty of time; we can patiently wait for our children to grasp and follow the vision God is preparing for them. That's why we're laying down these foundational preparations before we even begin to discuss the vision itself. Our patience provides an example of endurance, a model our children can imitate when they need to endure to the end of their journeys.

Beware of the temptation to step into one of their problems with a fix-it mentality. Be careful not to sweep away all encumbrances and hand them a step-by-step plan of action. Although in a true crisis our fathering responsibilities may demand such a move, we can usually exercise patience and allow God's gentle prodding to do its work.

When God led Israel, He was willing to show them many miracles, but He wasn't so willing to use supernatural acts to speed their journey. Patiently enduring their faltering steps, God cleansed a wayward people, weeding out an unfaithful generation to create a nation of souls who had no fond memories of the ways of the ungodly.

This kind of patience, standing by while a child stumbles, can make fathers squirm, but with a proper balance, even the most fix-it minded father can tolerate a few missteps. Here's the key. Allow faltering steps in areas that won't cause lasting damage, non-sinful areas that won't corrupt their hearts. Should he play tennis or basketball? Talk with him about the pros and cons of team versus individual sports and how each matches his talents and goals, but let him decide. Should she take Spanish or a second year of Latin? Go over with her the benefits of Latin in vocabulary skills and the open doors to ministry that Spanish offers, but let her make the choice. In other areas, however, you can bar the door. Regarding social activities, destructive habits, and countless other behaviors, you can still unequivocally spell out the big N.O.

God our Father gave you the Scriptures for guidance, often allowing you to solve your problems using the wisdom He has so graciously provided. As you advise your children, reflect God's permissive balance. Seek to be a sounding board, offering advice at appropriate times as you interact, allowing your children to come to wise conclusions by leading them in the proper direction. Each time you work out a problem, go over the advantages of various options, helping them understand the process of wise decision making.

In areas that involve no biblical principles that make a godly choice obvious, allow your children the freedom to act according to their desires, even if they don't line up with your own. If their choices prove right, you can later interact with them to evaluate the process after the fact, admitting that they chose well. If their choices prove wrong, however, an attitude of "I told you so" will crack their confidence to come to you with future issues.

Your daughter walks into the room, her books cradled in her arms and her shoulders sagging. "Dad, I don't think it's going to work out."

"The research project?"

"Yeah. Kaitlyn and Jessica are doing their part, but Laura's just riding along."

"Did you say anything to her?"

"Kaitlyn tried to tell her, and Laura said she'd do better, but she's not."

"Since you're the leader, I think you should try once more. Warn her that you have to report it to the teacher. If she doesn't do any better, you'll have to let her suffer the consequences."

"Yeah," she replies, nodding, "I guess you're right." After a short pause she adds, "Thanks, Dad, for not saying it."

"For not saying what?"

"For not saying, 'I told you so.' You're the one who said Laura wouldn't be good for our group."

With a wink and a nod, you pat her on the shoulder before she leaves the room, confident that she'll come to you again with her next problem.

Your patience will be rewarded, reaping an abundant harvest in your children's character. They'll be better prepared to face life because they've been trained to go through trials without your forced intervention. Foolish ways of thinking will be tested and found inadequate, even in their own eyes, as life itself burns away the chaff of faulty human thinking. As you exercise patience and restraint, they will exercise their decision-making abilities, making them more confident in themselves and more trusting in you and in God.

## ✧ Direction—Boundaries, Shelters, and Signposts

God put the Israelites in a rebellion-free zone, otherwise known as the wilderness highway to the Promised Land. In other words, the escapees from Egypt had a choice of doing things God's way or suffering death by various horrible tortures. Take your pick: obedience or fiery vipers, obedience or flesh-eating disease, obedience or huge cracks in the earth swallowing you up.

In our homes, although we don't threaten our children with plagues or poison, we are called to create a rebellion-free zone. Yes, we show compassion and patience in our role as guiding fathers, but we also establish clear direction, a system of values that may not be violated. Regarding morality, discipline, authority, respect, and other clearly defined biblical principles, it really should be our way or the highway with no allowance for rebellious dissent.

At the same time, however, a child should have a measure of freedom to move within well-established boundaries. Unfortunately, many parents want to give their children complete liberty, hoping that throwing open all options in all areas will help their young ones feel unshackled, with unrestrained freedom to make decisions on their own. A great danger lies in that path, for freedom in an untrained mind can lead to a different kind of slavery—chains of sin that will encircle a youngster who has not purged foolishness from his decision-making influences.

God did not allow the Israelites to scatter in the wilderness with each wanderer following his own moral compass. In like manner, we must not grant more freedom than wisdom allows simply because our children desire it. The guiding hand that rocked the cradle should not disappear into the background when the awkwardness of adolescence and the hormones of change bring a craving for auton-omy and peer acceptance. We must remain their primary guides during every stage of development, giving them unmistakable direc-tion, a single moral compass that we've found trustworthy, the pre-cepts of God's Word.

Let's break down our direction-steering actions into three con-crete activities: setting up boundaries, erecting shelters, and plant-ing signposts.

## Setting Up Boundaries

Boundaries are clearly defined behavior limits, and they are best set up with a philosophical foundation. In other words, a bound-ary can expand or contract if its underlying reason for existing isn't violated. It isn't made rigid by external symbols, yet its values are immovable.

For example, one boundary might be, "You may go to any G-rated movie. If a movie is rated PG, bring us a title and we'll look it up in a parent's guide. If it's PG-13, then either your mother or I must preview it first. R-rated or NC-17 rated movies are out of the question." The entertainment boundary is based on parental approval of content using a rating system as a guideline rather than on the rating system itself. The borders of the boundary, PG and PG-13, may shift, but the foundation of parental approval does not.

Another example might be, "You may not go to mixed-gender outings unless there is a reason for the get-together other than social interaction. If the outing has a service- or school-related function, then we'll decide based on the activity and who'll be chaperoning the event." In this case, the social boundary normally does not allow for boy-girl social contact, but it stretches to include approved functions.

As you can see, these boundaries are clearly defined, yet they can bend based on the circumstances or enlarged pending parental review. The underlying philosophy remains intact no matter how the boundary stretches.

## Erecting Shelters

Well-defined boundaries are important, but they create only one part of a family shelter. A safe harbor for children requires a more complete covering. Boundaries are limits of allowed behavior that keep those on the inside from drifting toward corrupting environments on the outside, but a shelter, in addition, has walls that prevent negative external influences from breaking in. At times, children might think of a shelter as a prison, but as the years go by, and as you carefully adapt your boundaries while maintaining their foundation, they'll learn the shelter's benefits. It's a place of refuge.

Though their peers may mock their values, home encouragement stokes the fires of acceptance and affirmation. For a guy, it's a recharging station. He can feel beaten down by the world and then come home to feed off his father's godly energy and wise counsel. For a girl, it's a fortress of protection. She can tell any male suitor, whether she likes him or not, to feel free to call her father, and she can come home feeling safe, not dreading the ring of the telephone.

A proper shelter is also not a monastery that prevents all inter-action with the outside world. A father should deliberately expose his children to opposing influences, guiding them with proper counterpoints to the subtle messages they may hear. These influ-ences might come in the form of political debates, philosophy text-books, or media images.

For example, three of my children—James, Arianna, and Caleb—attended a campus debate where the overwhelming message of the more able debater was that drugs should be legalized. They came home somewhat swayed toward that point of view. As we discussed the issue, I pointed out some flaws in the arguments and raised ques-tions they couldn't answer. Arianna became flustered, apparently dis-appointed that this new idea wasn't holding up well under scrutiny. I believe that her arsenal of arguments gave her a sense of freedom, a reason to hold to a point of view that differed from Dad's. As the viewpoint floundered, she actually left the room, not wanting to con-tinue the discussion. I decided I probably had been a little too force-ful with her, all too ready to skewer the opposition, not giving her time to see its flaws for herself. Her two brothers, however, perhaps because of their gender, had no trouble with the mental wrestling, and they willingly surrendered when they could not counter my arguments. My daughter came to me later and admitted the reason for her reticence, and I apologized for being too forceful.

Allowing a controlled attack on our family shelter ended up being a great opportunity to show its strength. The opposition was a known entity, limited, and easily defeated. My children experi-enced the alluring pull of a persuasive voice, to the point that it swayed their resolve. They returned to find that their home fires burned away arguments that seemed so sound at the debate, further establishing the foundation upon which our shelter was built. As these forays into the outside world continue, they'll learn to trust the wisdom from above over the wisdom of the world even if the world seems to have a better argument for a season.

## Planting Signposts

Besides boundaries and shelters, good direction also includes signposts, everyday rules that provide commands, warnings, and supervision within the boundaries. They're practical, directional, and planted with clear explanations of their underlying reasons. A Stop sign at the street corner is an obvious command, and we all know its reason for being there, to keep orderly flow at the intersection and to prevent collisions. Similarly, we give direct commands, such as "Eat your vegetables," "Look both ways before crossing the street," and "Keep your room clean." With each directive, we should be ready to give a reason, something more than just, "Daddy says so."

God has reasons for His commands, some to protect us, others to bring us blessings. Since we love Him, "God says so" is all we need to hear. We jump to obey. It helps, however, in the quiet of the evening, to hear God's voice speaking through His Word to explain His purpose in planting a signpost. When we learn of His protective hand and His blessings, we feel bathed in His love, making us even more ready to leap to obey the next command.

"Are you okay?" you call as you throw your bicycle down and run to your daughter's side.

She pulls on your hand and lifts herself up. Although her face is dirty and her cheek is bleeding, she seems okay. Her spill sent her body crashing to the ground and her head cracking against the pavement.

"Uh-huh. I think so. I feel a little dizzy."

You gingerly pull her helmet off and show it to her, putting your finger on a tiny crack that runs from one side to the other. "Good thing you had it on," you say, trying not to make it sound like, "I told you so."

As you walk your bikes home, she eyes her helmet dangling by its strap from your handlebar. She lets out a sigh and says, "You were right."

"About the helmet?"

"Uh-huh, that and something else."

"What else?"

She puts her free hand in yours. "You told me to wear it because you love me."

Don't underestimate the power of giving reasons for your commands. Although "Daddy says so" should be enough to bring obedience, it may foster robotic response, not loving, enthusiastic commitment. Let your signposts say more than Stop, Yield, and Speed Limit. Let them speak even more profoundly as each command whispers in the background, "I love you."

## ✧ Purpose—A Vision for Tomorrow

> Correct your son, and he will give you comfort;
> He will also delight your soul.
> Where there is no vision, the people are unrestrained,
> But happy is he who keeps the law. (Prov. 29:17, 18)

Much of our counsel is mandatory for our children. We physically stop them at the edge of their boundaries. We grab them from the storm and pull them into the shelter. We enforce the signposts, not allowing mere lip-service obedience. When they become adults, however, we transform into a guiding light that can be chosen or left behind. The choices we make as father-guide while they're young will carry great weight when they decide whether to seek our counsel when it's time to leave our protective shelter. Will they keep us close, or will they wave at us from afar, glad to be on the other side of a generational divide?

To bridge the gap, help your children capture a vision, a beacon that shines into the future. All the other qualities we discussed—compassion, patience, and direction—are mere preparation for this one encompassing purpose. A guiding vision will guarantee that, even after they leave your home, they'll have a reason for living, a plan that will help them create their own boundaries and chart their own course. And, remembering that you were the one who helped them lay out their plans, they'll come back to seek counsel from their coarchitect, the man who drew the foundation on the blueprint.

God had a purpose for the Israelites, that they should possess the Promised Land as His chosen and redeemed people. A vision of this land was their guiding force, a promise that helped them plant one more footstep in the shifting sands of the wilderness.

Children, too, need a vision. Without a vision, they'll have no way to channel their studies and activities toward their goals. A vision also provides a measure of sanity in everything they do, giving them strength to persevere in trying times.

As a father, you can help a child find and grab hold of a vision. Of course, since God provides the vision, you can expect that He is already preparing your children, giving them talents and strengths for the tasks that lie ahead. The key is to be aware. Look for special interests, activities that energize them. Do they find delight in nature? People? Numbers? As they get older, try to translate that interest into a vision by asking questions.

"So you really like bugs?"
"Yeah. They're cool. I like to cut them open to see what's inside."
"And you don't mind killing them to collect them?"
"Nah. If you get too many bugs, they can cause a lot of trouble."

Over time this young man might learn that he wants to become a surgeon, helping thousands with his healing scalpel, or he might capture a vision to become a pest specialist, teaching the poor how to increase farm production by eliminating damaging insects. It's important to keep an open mind as you delve into your children's strengths and talents.

I've had to do this kind of vision searching with one of my own children. My daughter, Arianna, has a vision to be a nurse, desiring to take on the servant attitude of Christ in that demanding profession. Still in high school, she has ordered her academic life around fulfilling the coursework required to eventually enter the school of nursing at the University of Florida. Even though she hates math, she knows that mastering it is necessary to make her vision a reality, so she racks her brain to make all the numbers come together. She even arranges her extracurricular activities in a way that makes her résumé well rounded and more attractive to the nursing school admissions office. She volunteers at a local hospital, she excels at the piano, and she plays competitive tennis, all with a single goal in mind, to serve Christ by serving others as a nurse. Whether she'll serve in a domestic hospital, as a missionary, or on a battlefield, she's not sure. Her vision will become focused as time goes on. For now, she has enough of a channel to guide her activities, giving her reason to take each new step in her journey.

As I said, I had to keep an open mind. Since my daughter also has excellent analytical and writing skills, I thought she might become a journalist or a research specialist. No, she wants to be a nurse. How can I argue with a vision? She enjoys being with people, so I assume her love for others will be her God-given aptitude enabling her to follow the course He has laid for her future. She has a vision; she has a plan to follow it; I'm a happy dad.

## ✦ Summary

God has a purpose for all the members of His kingdom. Discovering that purpose is the next step in our children's great journey. As fathers, we act as guides along the way, helping our children find their vision while watching over their steps as they traverse life's path. In following God's model for fatherly guidance we see four qualities in His loving hand: compassion, patience, direction, and purpose.

Compassion involves creating empathy with our children, understanding their fears and aspirations, letting them know we care. We don't belittle their emotions; we connect with them, giving them reason to have confidence to share them with us.

Patience is the gift of waiting. We may want to jump in and fix our children's problems, but that doesn't help them build inner strength and endurance. If a vision for our child's future is already in place, we may be tempted to constantly remind him of the goal, but in doing so, we risk making the vision an object of resentment, a hammer of dread. We need to trust in God's timing, giving our children visible symbols of their goal without beating them over the head with it.

Patience involves allowing our children to come to wise conclusions on their own, permitting them to make mistakes in areas that won't cause long-term damage, in issues that have no clear biblical principles to follow. We advise them, listing the pros and cons involved in their issues of concern, and we let them make their own decisions, building their confidence for the future.

Direction involves creating a system of values that may not be violated. We set up behavior boundaries, erect family shelters, and plant love-based signposts. Each of these methods for giving our children direction gives them a clear view of how to follow our guiding hand.

Our children need to have a purpose for life, a vision for the years ahead. As time goes on, we discern their talents and strengths and help them find how God wants to use them in His kingdom. This vision helps them channel their efforts, giving them a reason to pursue their interests, and creates a lasting path into the future.

# The Father as Warrior

## ✧ A Time for War

> The Lord will go forth like a warrior,
> He will arouse His zeal like a man of war.
> He will utter a shout, yes, He will raise a war cry.
> He will prevail against His enemies. (Isa. 42:13)

A salesman barked out a price, and two gritty barter-
ers haggled among a hundred others amid a cacophony of
bleating sheep and bellowing oxen, foul-smelling mer-
chandise made ready for sacrifice. At the market's edge,
unnoticed in the chaos, a man of peace knelt. With strong
fingers he wove strips of leather through a knot of twisted

rushes, binding them into a formidable whip. As he straightened his tall frame, he gazed at the beasts and their Jewish masters bustling across littered stone floors. With cattle hooves and peddlers' feet, they trampled a court set apart for the praying knees of Gentiles, pocketing spoils of thievery and leaving trails of animal dung, allowing no room for worship from the outcasts. With his whip in hand, anger burned as godly zeal rushed from his holy mind and into his tightening, muscular arms. For this man of peace, it was time for war.

War and Peace, the two great opposites. One plunges the world into chaos, spilling blood and extinguishing lives across the terrain as though they were nothing more than water and toy soldiers in a child's sandbox. The other brings order, calming the heat of battle like a drenching shower on an August afternoon. We long for peace and its blessings. We dread its loss. Yet we know that lasting peace often comes at the price of war. Such is the mystery of this timeless paradox.

There is a time for war and a time for peace; so says Solomon in Ecclesiastes. And it's a strange puzzle that God brings both conflict and tranquility to our nation, even to our front doors. Most of us will never have to charge across a field in the midst of a deadly metallic hail or fly bombing missions over hostile territories, but as fathers, we will have to go to war at some point and in some manner. Conflict is inevitable. In a culture that worships sex, entertainment, and possessions, we find ourselves battling against a rushing tide of sin on a daily basis, against the people who are corrupted by these fleshly indulgences, and against the practices of misplaced worship and false fidelity.

Our wars will probably never make the headlines; they're not the stuff of popular bravado or medaled heroism. Yet they sometimes require more courage than did the siege of Yorktown, more wisdom and thoughtful planning than preceded the landing on the beaches of Normandy. We fight battles for safety, freedom, and righteousness in our homes. Our struggles are both physical and spiritual, waged for the benefit of families, friends, and even strangers. And many of our enemies are hidden, either skulking behind their lines of defense or openly parading in the guise of friendship, clothed in our own uniforms.

Why are we called to combat? Because, as fathers, we're warriors for our families, God's arm of battle to protect our homes. God desires peace, but He often supplies it to us through the cleansing flood of war. And although we desire peace ourselves, we learn that reflecting God's fathering attributes often demands a sacrifice, in this case carrying out the sacred duty to answer a call to conflict. God's approach to assuring lasting peace may bring a shedding of tears, perhaps even blood, but shrinking away from the trumpet's call will fatally wound our standing as fathers.

Though God sometimes restrains Himself and seeks peaceful alternatives, we cannot shy away when He declares war. If we fall back, we will be cowards, proving that we don't love our families enough to provide the protection they need, demonstrating that we are not reflecting God's sacrificial heart for His people.

In this chapter, we'll look at when and why fathers should choose to wage war, both in the physical sense and in the spiritual. Though we long for peace, we'll learn to understand the need for war, how to fight with righteousness even while seeking peace and fostering the blessings of peace in all we do. We'll examine our duty to reflect God's peacemaking attributes in the next chapter.

Fathers, balancing war and peace is a delicate operation, one that will bring great harm if we tilt too much to one side or the other. Let's learn how we can reflect our heavenly Father's attributes as a God who wages war, thereby creating real peace that will abide forever.

## ✧ Peace, Peace, but There Is No Peace

Most of the time we live in relative peace. We go through our daily routines without even a proverbial bump in the road of our everyday lives. Peace is to be highly desired; it offers comfort—the assurance of God's blessings, as the psalmist says, "The Lord will bless His people with peace" (29:11). And Jesus said, "Peace I leave with you; My peace I give to you; not as the world gives, do I give to you" (John 14:27). Long stretches of peace, however, can create a problem. Peace, by its very nature, calms the soul as it croons a lilting song of relaxation. With rest comes released tension, and the watchful eye is tempted to stray from tedious sentry duty; the sword of defense may fall to the side.

During these idyllic times, the desire to maintain peace can become paramount, even when going to war is the more righteous option. Peace can lull us to sleep; it can even dull our senses. It can make us trust in peace itself, believing in its perfect wholeness even as it erodes on every side.

God warned about this unrealistic faith in peace through His prophet, Jeremiah.

> For from the least of them even to the greatest of them,
> Everyone is greedy for gain,
> And from the prophet even to the priest
> Everyone deals falsely.
> And they have healed the brokenness of My people superficially,
> Saying, 'Peace, peace,'
> But there is no peace. (Jer. 6:13, 14)

Fathers, our first lesson is that we'll never have perfect peace until our enemy is completely defeated. In fact, on many fronts, we're constantly at war, and the man who is unaware of the battle is sure to lose it. Evil lurks outside our doors; it can filter into our homes through cracks we allow in our defenses. Most of us would gladly tackle any physical intruder that breaks into our homes, be it man or monster, and risk our lives to protect our loved ones, but some of the most dangerous invaders are not so easily seen. They threaten peace and safety through stealth and through spiritual and emotional attacks. Because of this ever-present menace, we should always be on guard, always in a state of alert, not allowing superficial peace to lull us into a false sense of security.

What are these dangers, the intruders at our doors? Since their presence takes many forms and their modes of attack vary, it isn't easy to categorize threats to peace, making any list we might create incomplete. We will, however, discuss a few of the most notorious threats to our homes.

> For our struggle is not against flesh and blood, but against the rulers, against the powers, against the world forces of this darkness, against the spiritual forces of wickedness in the heavenly places. (Eph. 6:12)

The apostle Paul teaches that our most important struggles are spiritual, so he implores us to put on spiritual armor to ready ourselves for combat. He is, of course, correct; our most crucial conflicts are not fought with fists or by throwing sticks and stones. What we have to realize, however, is that spiritual battles can take place in the physical realm. Our spiritual enemies can be personified in a number of physical entities, and we may have to confront them bodily as well as spiritually.

For example, one group of enemies, according to the Scripture above, is "the powers" or "the authorities." Paul was likely referring to a demonic hierarchy that threatens us, but although they may be a spiritual menace, their attacks can come through the world's system, as it says, "the world forces of this darkness." Satan is called the prince of the power of the air (see Eph. 2:2) and the god and ruler of this world (see 2 Cor. 4:4 and John 12:31). There is little doubt that the ruler can use his earthly minions as an attacking army.

And in keeping with Satan's desire to be the ruler of this world, he tries to destroy the islands of rebellion against him in the land he claims as his domain, the bastions of resistance we call Christian homes. A father is the head of a local command post, receiving his commission from on high; therefore, the attacking force will first try to destroy this earthly commander in chief.

The enemy's most effective way to achieve victory is to assail the authority of the father, the head of the home, and he attempts this in at least three ways. The first is to attack him personally, to tempt him to sin in order to destroy his integrity and thereby his authority to command. This is exactly what Satan did to Jesus, his first salvo in trying to short-circuit Christ's ministry. So it should come as no surprise when a battle looms on the horizon that temptations to sin become more frequent and more powerful.

The second line of attack is to incite rebellion in the ranks, to tempt one of the children to rise up against his father's authority. If the father fails to maintain control by allowing open challenges to go without correction, his power to command slips in the eyes of his remaining troops, the siblings of the wayward child, thus undermining everything the Christian home stands for. With authority eroding, the father's precepts crumble in turn, and the island of resistance against Satan is swallowed up from the inside out.

The third method is to infiltrate the home with other authorities, respected leaders from the outside who might challenge a father's standing. I'm sure we've all heard about schoolteachers telling students to ignore their parents' old-fashioned dogma, and we've seen government erode the rights of parents, assuming the state can better care for all children. Hollywood and sports celebrities become heroes in the eyes of the young, and morality in these groups is frequently lower than that of most rodent communities. We've even seen pastors try to excuse sin and relax standards that parents try to uphold. And finally, we often see the media portraying fathers as cave dwellers, clueless relics of the past who have no idea what's going on, who exercise no control over any situation that really matters. Each of these influences undermines the authority of a father, especially if his children look to him as a model for behavior or as a reliable source of truth.

So in these cases you can see how an enemy's attack can be launched as an insidious assault, quiet, doing damage without firing an audible shot. Even while everything seems at peace, war constantly rages in the spiritual realm. Be on the lookout for signs of impending battle. Do you perceive an unusual assault on yourself, people trying to get you to compromise your integrity? Is a child resisting your authority? Is he citing other authorities in response to your directives? Are there influences filtering in that would bring about these evils? It's up to you to root out corrupting influences before they can bear their rotten fruit.

The battle to uphold authority is merely one of many you'll have to fight. Because of the various modes of attack, how do you know when to wage war and when to hold back? How do you prepare for battle? Physical and spiritual diligence combine to make us ready, and we'll look at this overriding principle in the following sections.

Although real peace is realized only in heaven, you can allow your family to enjoy a time of relative comfort and safety. If you're always prepared, never letting your watchful eyes stray from your borders, you can give your children an earthly view of heaven's peace. Don't believe, however, that there is peace if your borders are being eaten away or if an enemy has planted seeds of discord in your fields. There is a time for war. Let's explore how to discern when its season has arrived.

## ✧ War or Peace?

You have heard that it was said, "An eye for an eye, and a tooth for a tooth." But I say to you, do not resist him who is evil; but whoever slaps you on your right cheek, turn to him the other also. (Matt. 5:38, 39)

With the words of Christ so vividly portraying a man of peace, one who would even turn away from a direct assault, why would we ever try to justify an act of aggression? Did Jesus intend for us to passively allow any and all attackers to bring evil upon us and our families?

Jesus' own words and actions demonstrate that the answer is clearly no, and our Lord also helps us understand the times and reasons for raising our defenses and even when to go on the offensive. With a whip in hand He cleansed the temple, with the sword of the Spirit in His voice He cast out demons, and with the wisdom of the ages He confronted and vanquished a host of pharisaical hypocrites. Jesus was clearly a man of action.

But when do we turn the other cheek? And under what circumstances are we obligated to brandish our weapons?

When a man strikes you on the cheek, he has injured or offended only one person, you. He has threatened neither family nor friend, stolen neither money nor property, and has violated neither rights nor privileges of any other person. Since love demands selflessness, it's appropriate, even commanded, that you take no revenge and allow room for God to answer this man's violence (see Rom. 12:19). Personal assaults, therefore, demand a peaceful response and a soft answer.

A person who injures someone else, however, invites the wrath of the righteous. Jesus never resisted violence against Himself, remaining silent under a hail of whips, fists, and words. But when others were threatened, He came to their aid, sometimes with a furious assault, and He will come again bearing a punishing sword. "And I saw heaven opened; and behold, a white horse, and He who sat upon it is called Faithful and True; and in righteousness He judges and wages war" (Rev. 19:11).

If your wife or child is in danger, a turn of your cheek becomes an evil, cowardly act. If an enemy attacks your home with toxic influences, such as drugs, pornography, or destructive ideas, it's your duty to unsheathe your sword. You are a father; you are called to provide for your family. What kind of provider would you be if you gave a child his daily bread and then allowed a predator to poison his mind and lead him into hell? Only a faithless fool would be so callous, as the Scripture says, "But if anyone does not provide for his own, and especially for those of his household, he has denied the faith, and is worse than an unbeliever" (1 Tim. 5:8).

Our warlike defense arises in two arenas, the physical and the spiritual. Most of us have no problem dealing with the physical. Our very hormones testify that we are wired to fight, especially when we feel the rage that surges through us when someone attacks one of our children.

One day, when Arianna was about eight years old, I sat in the back row of our church during a congregational meeting, peering at her from time to time as she played in the churchyard. A boy about her age approached her and began kicking her viciously with his booted foot. I leaped to my feet and dashed out the door with my wife, Susie, running close behind. With a strong hand I clenched the front of the boy's shirt and yanked him away, literally picking him up off the ground with my grasp while my wife took care of our daughter. If Arianna's attacker had been an adult, I have no doubt I would have treated him much more roughly. As it was, I merely confronted the boy verbally, putting the fear of God into his soul with my firm grip and my ferocious countenance.

With an attack underway, this was no time for peaceful negotiation or sweet-sounding words of reconciliation. I had to act with physical aggression to prevent further injury to Arianna, both at that moment, and for future encounters, at least from this juvenile antagonist. He knew at that moment and forevermore that if he bothered my daughter, he would have to deal with me.

A physical attack demands a physical response when the assault is on someone in your charge who is too weak to defend herself. If you allow injury because of your hesitance to act, either because of fear or because of a desire to make peace, not only will you have broken faith with your brood, you will have destroyed their trust in you. It is your sacred duty to protect and defend them, and a cowardly miscarriage of that responsibility will make them look at you with new eyes. They will see weakness. Instead of a bold knight, they will see a cowering dog. You have spoken bravely in the light of day, but what will happen the next time an evil shadow appears? You might as well not bother with tucking them in at night. It will no longer bring a sigh of security, for you will have proven you will not defend them in the darkness. And since you, in their minds, are a reflection of heavenly protection, will God defend them?

Spiritual war differs from the physical only in the nature of the battlefields. The front lines of these wars exist in invisible realms, though they're often manifested in concrete reality. In other words, spiritual forces can work in human vessels. For example, a philosophy of evil that attacks the wisdom of Scripture may appear in the guise of a charismatic teacher who praises evolutionary theory and ridicules any form of creationism. And to this we must respond with vigorous debate or even personal confrontation. The spirit of lust may seek fuel in magazine photographs or Internet images, requiring us to physically shut off their flow to our homes or even to our communities through protest or economic boycott of a particular store.

Spiritual battles may not always reveal a physical presence, and in those cases our only weapons will be spiritual. In the previous example, even if the sewage of pornography is halted, the battle may continue in the mind for years, for the scars implanted by this deadly weapon can replay their images over and over. After our physical confrontation comes to an end, we must reach for our greatest invisible weapon, prayer, for this spirit can only be eradicated as we wage war on our knees.

Fathers, there is evil in this world, and it's up to us to discern its presence and destroy its power. We can't pretend everything's fine, that there is peace when there is no peace. Jesus promised we would have tribulation, so we'd better prepare for its arrival. But we can always take courage—our Lord has overcome the world. As we rise up to defend our families, our swords will be energized by God's holy presence, for He has promised to be with us until the end of the age.

## ✧ Preparation for War

> Therefore, take up the full armor of God, that you may be able to resist in the evil day, and having done everything, to stand firm. Stand firm therefore, having girded your loins with truth, and having put on the breastplate of righteousness, and having shod your feet with the preparation of the gospel of peace; in addition to all, taking up the shield of faith with which you will be able to extinguish all the flaming missiles of the evil one. And take the helmet of salvation, and the sword of the Spirit, which is the word of God. (Eph. 6:13–17)

We pray for peace, and even while we pray, we prepare for war. As we exercise our peaceful options in order to avert confrontation, we make ourselves ready should they fail. In the previous section we categorized different kinds of attacks and the counterattacks we're obligated to provide. Each of these defenses requires its unique method of preparation.

### *Physical Preparation*

It's no shame to lack the physique of the musclebound models that grace the covers of fitness magazines and romance novels. The amount of exercise required to build and maintain that kind of body is enormous, and few have the hours needed to devote to such a narrowly focused regimen, one that often leads to self-absorption and body worship. We can, however, set aside time for exercise, in concert with our other disciplines, to maintain strength and endurance, always remembering to keep it in balance with our mental and spiritual workouts.

God has gifted men with body structure and hormonal makeup that allow for rapid muscular development. It really doesn't take much exercise to make a significant difference in your physical abilities. If you've been sedentary for a long time, put your body to a test. Jump rope for about fifteen minutes a day, lift weights for ten, and then drop down for thirty pushups. In just a few days you'll see and feel a dramatic impact on your body. No, not just soreness, a feeling of hardening muscles and energizing flow. It may take you a while to build up to this level, and you may want to exceed those goals over time, but it's important to set aside some time for physical development and maintenance. It's one of your preparation categories, one of your obligations of love.

When you're able to pick up your toddler and hoist her high into the air without struggle or pain, she'll feel security in your strength. When you embrace your wife and fold her into arms hardened by your recent workout, she'll appreciate your efforts and joyfully take shelter within your grasp. You don't have to be Hercules to bring security to your family, but if you show your loving protection in this visible way, they'll have more confidence, and so will you, every time you have to walk down a dark street or meet a stranger in a lonely place.

It is true that some men are not able to do any of these exercises, whether from handicap, illness, or injury. They're no less masculine, no less obligated to build and show what strength they can. If this is your situation, do whatever you can to build strength, and God will supply whatever protection you may not be able to provide.

## *Spiritual Preparation*

Lonely places can be found in nonphysical realms. There may be dark days in our homes, times of spiritual attack, and our preparation for these requires discipline that goes beyond the physical. As Paul taught in Ephesians, "Therefore, take up the full armor of God, that you may be able to resist in the evil day, and having done everything, to stand firm" (6:13). Many authors have written on this passage, explaining each piece of armor and its use. Indeed, the wisdom in the apostle's instruction could fill an entire book. I would like to focus, however, on two points, Paul's assumption of readiness and his command to stand firm.

Notice the phrase "having done everything." The tense indicates that Paul assumes prior preparation, that the reader has already clapped on the specific pieces of armor. For example, Paul says, "having girded your loins with truth," indicating that the warrior made himself ready beforehand. The bottom line is that we cannot stand firm in war without having taken the time to prepare during times of peace. We cannot expect to notice the fires of war being kindled and then hurriedly strap on our armor in time to battle successfully. We have to keep it on at all times, knowing that a battle may always be at hand. We wear it to work. We wear it to bed. We wear it in the shower. Spiritual armor never rusts.

How can you assure that your armor is on and ready for battle? Every moment you conscientiously study God's Word you wrap another girding layer of truth around your loins. As you walk in holiness day by day, your breastplate of righteousness thickens its defense against Satan's darts. Each act of deep, abiding love for others dresses your feet with the preparation of the gospel of peace.

Beware of putting on false armor. A mere attitude of righteousness that magically appears in times of war is a counterfeit breastplate. It is hypocrisy, a transparent vest that will fail in the heat of battle. A hastily concocted affection will not protect your feet. It wilts when carrying the gospel becomes fraught with danger.

If you take up the shield of faith, and its mettle is not already proven through meditation on God's protective acts through the annals of history, the first volley of Satan's flaming missiles will pierce and consume it.

When you take the Sword of the Spirit, if you're not already skilled in its use, it will be your undoing as your enemy wrests it from your grasp and uses it against you. And if the helmet of salvation is an imitation, not the true, impenetrable skull of a Christian warrior, you won't be able to charge courageously into battle, for the fear of man and the fear of death will penetrate your helmet's veneer and overwhelm your trembling mind. If you know you belong to God and have a home in heaven, you wear the confidence of fearlessness. When you know your armor is strong and well mounted, you stand firm in the strength of God's might.

## ✧ Waging War

> And I saw heaven opened; and behold, a white horse, and He who sat upon it is called Faithful and True; and in righteousness He judges and wages war. (Rev. 19:11)

In order to follow God's example of waging war in righteousness, we need to understand His methods, how He would execute battles in every stage of conflict. God does not enter into war lightly, and His wrath, being kindled in righteousness and withdrawn through His own mercy, lasts for only a season.

Your first step when faced with danger to your home is to make entreaty with your enemy, requesting or demanding that the threat be taken away, assuming the danger isn't already causing damage or threatening immediate harm. It's too late for entreaty if an enemy is already aggressively attacking. When there is hope for peace, however, there is no need to do battle if a simple request can avert a war. Just as God used Jonah to appeal to the people of Nineveh to repent of their wickedness, so should a father discuss terms of peace with his enemies.

In the earlier examples of spiritual warfare—the battles with the teacher of evolution and the seller of pornography—there's an option to entreat. You could ask the evolutionist teacher to fairly balance the two sides of the origins debate. You could ask the local store manager to refuse to stock and sell pornography. Fostering peace through dialogue is the ideal alternative to war, and we'll go deeper into this concept in the next chapter.

The second step of righteous warfare is conducting the battle. God does not call you to wield either physical or spiritual weapons with the idea of seeking revenge or killing your enemies. Your goal is to stop the enemy's attack, and you can leave revenge and ultimate destruction to God. Yes, it is true that the only way to stop an enemy may be to destroy him completely, and God may call you to a more aggressive campaign, but that should not be your primary goal when you enter battle.

Again, look at one of our examples. Although getting the evolutionist fired may be the only way to get him to stop trying to persuade your children of his philosophy, your goal is to pressure him through other means, whether debate, an appeal to the sacredness of family boundaries, or a petition to higher authorities to forbid his practices. You may eventually have to appeal for his removal, but your first volley is one of restraint.

This example can serve to remind us that God will sometimes go to war on our behalf, allowing us to sit and watch His salvation work. He may enlist others to fight for our cause when the battlefield is not within our reach or when someone else is more skilled in a particular area of conflict. God may move the superintendent of schools to apply pressure on the teacher, or God may call a legislator to take up the cause in the halls of state government.

In the case of the store carrying pornography, you should not bring torches and bulldozers to destroy your enemy's place of business. The proprietor might be persuaded to your side if you present him with evidence that pornography is damaging to his community, that its easy accessibility increases rape, prostitution, and organized crime activity in every area it becomes entrenched. And God may bring the issue straight to the manager's heart through damaging circumstances that prove your evidence. Perhaps his store or one of his customers will be robbed, giving evidence of the evil element pornography attracts.

The bottom line is that righteous warfare does not seek first the death of an enemy; it seeks to end his aggression as you fight with weapons designed not for mass destruction but rather for neutralizing the power of the enemy. It seeks his conversion as you attempt to remove the enemy's spirit of rebellion through your love-motivated actions.

The third step in war, after a victorious, if not decisive, battle is over, is to parley, to make an invitation to discuss terms of your enemy's surrender. The simple act of making a defense against your enemy could alter his view; it could help him see that you are not going to cower in a corner. When he witnesses your resolve, he might be willing to accept an offer of peace on your terms. In our examples, you could ask for a written pledge from the teacher to balance the evidence for creation with that of evolutionary theory. Similarly, a letter from the local store promising to refrain from selling pornography could bring an end to that conflict.

Finally, when the enemy has surrendered and is no longer a threat, it's time to invite reconciliation, the restoration of fellowship, if such fellowship previously existed. Or you could try to establish a new relationship. These relationships are only possible if the enemy has repented, because true reconciliation is only achieved if the former enemy is no longer a danger. A simple truce, the laying down of arms by the enemy, is often enough to establish and maintain peace. The problem is that without complete surrender, without the giving up of their weapons and philosophy, you will always have to stay on alert. There will never be lasting, restful peace with an unrepentant enemy.

Unless the evolutionist becomes a creationist, you'll have to keep an eye of vigilance on his teaching. His heart still trusts in science, not in God. If the store manager cleans out his pornography section simply because he's convinced of its negative economic influence, he could restock the shelves if another store fills its aisles with his old customers. Only when his heart is converted to disdain evil at any cost will you be able to find complete satisfaction in his surrender.

Establishing a relationship with your former enemy requires real compassion, the kind God has for His creation. The book of Jonah shows how God began the steps of warfare and how His initial entreaty worked to forestall destruction. After Jonah's warning, the people of Nineveh repented, demonstrating faith when they could have scoffed at the strange prophet. Jonah became upset when God forgave Nineveh and held back His wrath. He lacked godly compassion, a crucial component of righteous warfare. As God said to Jonah,

> And should I not have compassion on Nineveh, the great city in which there are more than 120,000 persons who do not know the difference between their right and left hand, as well as many animals? (Jon. 4:11)

Seek not the blood of your enemies; long for them to drink the living water (see John 4:10). Seek not revenge on your attackers; beg for their reconciliation with God (see 2 Cor. 5:20). Seek not the damnation of your foes; endure for their salvation (see 2 Tim. 2:10).

Every battle has an end, though it rages through the long, bloody day. The sun sets on every war, whether it is fought with words of power or weapons of steel. When darkness covers the battlefield and soldiers gather their wounded and their dead, both winners and losers know that the sun shall soon rise. What will the dawning of a new day reveal? The righteous will not fear the light's arrival, while those who have battled on the side of evil cringe at the first brightening ray.

There are no secrets when God's Spirit searches the hearts of men. When the battle is over, will our deeds match our intentions? May God find within each of our breasts the righteous heart of a warrior, the valiant core of the father made in the image of God, the soul of a man who flees not from the light of the new day.

## ✧ Summary

After trying to establish and keep peace in his home, a father is sometimes called by God to battle for his family. As fathers, we watch for signs of battle, both physical and spiritual. Even the spiritual forces may appear in physical form as they try to weaken our authority through insidious means. Through our preparedness, our families can enjoy peaceful times, knowing that Dad is always on guard.

Knowing when to hope for peace and when to go to battle takes great discernment. Personal assaults can be managed with a turn of the cheek, but if someone or something threatens family or friends, a father is obligated to defend and protect with his own aggressive force. Physical attacks invite immediate physical response, while spiritual attacks may require both physical and spiritual intervention, using prayer and God's Word as our weapons.

Our preparation for battle is twofold—physical readiness through bodily exercise and spiritual strength through knowing God and His Word. We must diligently use our times of peace to prepare for times of war, because when war comes, it will be too late to break out our fitness gear.

The act of waging war in righteousness involves four steps; entreaty, battle, parley, and reconciliation. Entreaty hopes for peace and offers terms to allow peaceful times to continue. Righteous battle seeks to disarm the enemy and prevent him from causing damage to our homes. Parley is an invitation for your enemy to surrender without further conflict. It allows the enemy to give up when he sees that his destruction may be imminent if he continues his aggressive ways. Reconciliation allows us to have a relationship with our former enemy, if he repents and seeks forgiveness. Desiring his conversion is an act of love, as Jesus said, "Love your enemies, and pray for those who persecute you" (Matt. 5:44). Though our enemy sometimes forces us to fight, we can still seek his ultimate good, which can only come through complete surrender.

# The Father as Peacemaker

## ✧ Overcoming Evil

If possible, so far as it depends on you, be at peace
with all men. Never take your own revenge, beloved,
but leave room for the wrath of God, for it is written, "Vengeance is Mine, I will repay," says the Lord.
"But if your enemy is hungry, feed him, and if he is
thirsty, give him a drink; for in so doing you will heap
burning coals upon his head." Do not be overcome by
evil, but overcome evil with good. (Rom. 12:18–21)

Once upon a time, Magnus, the strongest man in the
world, went to war along with his king's army. With

Magnus in their ranks, the Araenean troops swelled with confidence, blazing through the Panthean army like raging fire over tinder-dry grass. With the evildoers beaten back, the Araeneans marched into the enemy's capital city in triumph, taking their emperor and his wicked senate into captivity for later trial. For years the wicked emperor had enslaved the people, forcing them to turn over all their industry to him, paying them a pittance in return.

Magnus, his great voice lifted as a resounding trumpet, shouted a proclamation of freedom to the people. Just as he finished, a young male villager walked up and spat in Magnus' face. "Go away, you beast, you pig! We have no food, no money to buy even a loaf of bread for our children. Now you've taken away our emperor, our only means to sell our goods to the kingdoms around us."

The crowd held its breath as it watched Magnus the Great draw his long sword from its scabbard. The young man's eyes grew wide, and he stood petrified in his place. Everyone in the city expected to see the smaller man's head rolling on the ground in a matter of seconds.

Magnus lowered his massive body to one knee, bowed his head, and presented the sword to the man. "The sword is yours. Take it. You may strike me down with it and destroy the one who has brought you freedom, or you may sell it to gain money with which you may feed your children."

In stunned silence, the crowd waited, watching the bowed Magnus and the trembling citizen who now held the warrior's sword. In shame, the smaller man placed the sword on the ground and disappeared into the throng.

Magnus' squire ran to his master and snatched up the sword while others gathered around. Slowly the warrior lifted himself up and took his weapon.

"Why?" the squire asked. "Why didn't you cut off his worthless head? Surely he deserved it. And you're the strongest man in the world. Surely you could have done it with ease."

"For two reasons," Magnus replied. "Because, although he deserved it, he and his children need mercy more than they need punishment. And because," he added, sliding his sword back into its scabbard, "I am the strongest man in the world."

The most powerful of warriors is the man who has the strength to show restraint, to withhold his attack for the purpose of peace. Anyone can charge thoughtlessly into battle with revenge in his heart, but it takes a much stronger man to cast away the sword of retribution and instead put on a coat of mercy and share its loving warmth with an enemy.

Some people may deserve revenge; they may have committed acts so evil they ought to die. But the gospel teaches us not to deliver a just punishment to everyone who deserves it. Yes, evil must be vanquished, but it is not the sword that brings the most profound change.

Here is the gospel modeled in its simplicity. At one time we were at enmity with God, His enemies, in a sense, because we were in rebellion against His kingdom. God did not give us the punishment we deserved, and instead willingly sacrificed His Son in our place, bringing peace between Him and us. In the same way, we can sacrifice by withholding punishment from our enemies, instead destroying the enmity between us and our foes with the weapons of good and righteous conduct. Since we've been shown mercy we didn't deserve, we have a duty to pass that mercy along to our enemies. It was freely given to us; freely we pour it out on others.

Fathers, we can't deny that this plan of peace worked for God, our perfect model of a father. It can also work for us. Both inside and outside our homes, we can strive for peace without resorting to conflict, teaching our children how to overcome evil by doing good, transforming our peaceful acts into spiritual weapons that confound those who would do us harm. As we'll see, turning the cheek to avoid violence is almost always the most effective way to infiltrate and convert an evil heart.

Evildoers understand the ways of violence. When they provoke, they expect retaliation. When they gouge an eye, they expect their opponents to gouge theirs in return. If we, however, make a conscious decision not to respond in kind, we might inspire a new concept in their thinking. At first, a soft answer in response to a violent assault is maddening to the violent party. As Paul said, it heaps burning coals on his head. He doesn't know how to deal with unexpected, undeserved love. His first reaction may be rage as he comprehends that you've made a fool out of him, having exposed him as the unreasonable aggressor. In his heart, however, he may marvel at your inner strength, restraint he has never possessed.

Only the most callous of fools would not be able to perceive some sort of nobility in your peaceful ways. Beasts such as those would probably interpret your peaceful turn of the cheek as an act of cowardice and then try to dominate you with even more force. It's possible that this kind of person will never be converted by love, and you may have to leave it up to God to exact the revenge due an unreasoning savage. With a fool like this, if he continues his assault, you may be forced to fight, either defending yourself until you can safely leave or beating him back until he's no longer willing to attack. In other words, if your attempts at peace fail, you may have to go to war.

Some people have never witnessed God's amazing grace. They only understand the law of retribution, the natural law of man. "An eye for an eye and a tooth for a tooth" is a sensible code to them; it creates a system of behavior that protects and defends against harm. The problem is that, although this law is a deterrent against acts of evil, it can never change a person's heart. It punishes, but it does not deliver from evil. Not only is it incapable of rescuing anyone from slavery, it keeps people locked in chains. Through constant practice, it embeds a principle of retribution without mercy.

Acts of evil are born from cold hearts of granite, stony deserts of rebellion God desires to renew, as He said, "I will give you a new heart and put a new spirit within you; and I will remove the heart of stone from your flesh and give you a heart of flesh" (Ezek. 36:26). Exchanging one evil act for another has never softened a hardened heart; it cannot bring conversion. There is only one weapon that can break through a mind that knows only the law of nature—a different law, a principle that defies the embedded doctrine. Doing good in the face of evil violates the law of nature; it upsets the balance of "an eye for an eye." What is deserved is not carried out, leaving a void in the expected chain of justice, leaving the enemy wondering.

Witnessing an act of sacrifice when revenge is expected can awaken a dormant seed, the imprint of God and His perfect law that was once planted within (see James 1:21–25). Mercy can come as such a surprise that an aggressor may search for a reason for what seems unreasonable. He sees true love manifested, good replacing evil, and this spark of grace may kindle a fire that causes him to explore the meaning of this strange new law.

A classic children's story has illustrated this concept beautifully. In "How the Grinch Stole Christmas," the Grinch took everything related to Christmas in all of *Who*-ville, and when he lugged everything up to the mountain peak to dump it, he waited to hear the sounds of *Whos* wailing over the loss of their annual goodies. But how did the *Whos* react? They did not return evil for evil, crying out against injustice or retaliating. Instead, they met in the center of the village, joining hands as always, and they celebrated another year together. The Grinch was amazed at this unexpected show of love. His deformed heart grew three sizes, and he charged back into *Who*-ville, returning everything he had stolen. The *Whos*, of course, forgave the Grinch and welcomed him with open arms.

Unexpected grace is a beloved theme in great classics, as well. In *Les Misérables,* for example, Jean Valjean was converted through the bishop's unexpected gift of silver candlesticks in the face of Jean's treachery. In the Bible, King Saul stopped tormenting David, at least for a while, when David proved his loyalty by merely cutting off a piece of Saul's robe when he could have killed him. And countless Christians through the centuries have similarly melted the hearts of their tormentors through acts of kindness and mercy.

The act of overcoming evil with good, although an ancient philosophy, will never decay or lose its power. Although some people are too callous to feel its penetrating heat, love works to promote peace better than any war, because it changes hearts. Love is a powerful tool, applicable both in our homes and out in the world, and as we look at how it can bring peace in both venues, let us ingrain its passion for peace in our hearts.

## ✧ Peace within the Home

> Peace I leave with you; My peace I give to you; not as the world gives, do I give to you. Let not your heart be troubled, nor let it be fearful. (John 14:27)

Though strife and conflict rage all around, if we have peace at home, we can persevere in our struggles, knowing there's a haven of rest at the end of the day. Some of us can relate to home as a heaven on earth, as we rest from our labors in the embrace of a loving wife and respectful children. Others, however, see their homes as yet another place of conflict, with any number of crises arising on a daily basis, battles between husband and wife, rebellious behavior from children, and the constant bickering of sibling rivalry, all contributing to a household hell.

Fathers, there's no foolproof cure, no automatic way to ensure a cease-fire on the home front. For our part, we can strive to be at peace, making sure we never launch the first attack or even answer in kind when provoked. We cannot, however, take control of someone else's will; there's no external switch in another person's mind that we can tweak and force a peaceful attitude. Still, our principle of overcoming evil with good will go a long way toward soothing tempers and avoiding conflict. And lasting peace starts with your beloved bride.

## Peace with Your Wife

Being at peace with your wife is the foundation of peace in your home. A simple truce, an agreement to refrain from fighting, isn't enough to secure the blessings of long-lasting peace. When two become one flesh, both spiritually and physically, over time they can become of one mind as well. Years of loving communication can blend two individuals into an indivisible unit, making them a team in all aspects of life.

Being at war with your wife is unnatural. It violates every principle of God's order, his model for salvation and fellowship. It is acid instead of milk in your cereal. It is Hitler teaching Sunday school. It is Jesus making an obscene gesture. Tragically, many of you experience this heartbreak, this grotesque twisting of all that is right and good. The one you vowed to love, honor, and cherish has become an alien, foreign in both mind and spirit.

Whether such alienation is your fault, hers, or a combination, it's time to end the war, to mend the damage, to restore trust and oneness. You will not, and cannot, be a good father unless you're at peace with the mother of your children. The caustic blood of conflict and turmoil, whether visible or hidden, will ooze out and filter into their minds like radiation from a faulty nuclear power plant. At the very least, the absence of married unity will swallow up peace like a vacuum. The void in the family foundation will give your children no model of harmony upon which to stand.

From simple clashes to outright battles, your plan should be the same; overcome evil with good, whether evil is defined as outright malice and hatred or simply stress, fatigue, and anxiety. Any source of tension can build if her first volley is answered with one of your own. Don't let that happen; catch the painful words in a soft glove and let them slide into God's hands.

For example, if your wife takes issue with something you've done, and her initial contact is aggressive, respond with a soft answer, owning up to any responsibility you have in the matter. On the mundane side, suppose your toddler knocked over the garbage pail, spilling greasy chicken all over the floor, and the cat dragged the chicken skin to a hiding place you can smell but can't seem to find. Your wife, who's now trying to hold the slippery toddler before he tramps grease all over the house, glares at you and shouts, "Why can't you ever remember to take the garbage out?"

Whether you're guilty or not has no bearing on the tone of your answer. Your reply should be bathed in love. "Honey," you might say, reaching for Junior, "I'm sorry about the mess. Let me clean him up, and I'll come back and mop the floor." This kind of attitude disarms the one who's upset, giving her no good reason to fire another salvo. Later, when her nerves are calmed and she's more relaxed, you can discuss what ought to be done about garbage duty.

Undoubtedly, there are far more severe volleys that might be aimed your way. Your wife may not be a Christian; she may have no desire to work toward peace in your home. She could follow the prototype of Solomon's nightmare mate so eloquently described in Proverbs. "It is better to live in a corner of the roof than in a house shared with a contentious woman" (21:9). But whether your wife is Pollyanna or the Wicked Witch of the West, a soft answer will work wonders no matter how mundane or serious the crisis might be.

Above all, never, ever fire the first shot of evil. If you do, then you're the instigator of war, the malevolent party in the conflict. You might as well put this book down now and write the word "Unfaithful" or "Hypocrite" on your forehead. None of this advice will benefit you if you're unwilling to sacrifice, to allow the painful arrows of discord to pass through your mind without launching a counterattack or later firing a vengeful strike when her defenses are down.

Fathers, for the sake of your families, for the sake of glorifying God and His model of salvation, be at peace with your wives. It is impossible to overestimate the importance of this counsel. Wars eventually kill, and the collateral damage may include little innocent ones who look to you as the one who establishes peace and safety in their homes. If you can't show love to a child's mother, if you can't keep that sacred vow, what kind of man are you?

## *Peace with Your Children*

Using this pattern of maintaining peace with your wife will give you a foundation for peace with your children. As they watch your gentle manner with the woman you love, they'll see this behavior as a natural way of life. And when you carry peace into your conversations with them, they'll perceive an unkind response to be as strange as a kazoo in a symphony orchestra.

It's possible, however, even in this environment, for a child to spew out a hurtful statement during a time of passion or crisis. Although a harsh word from a child should always be considered a disobedient or rebellious act, we don't have to respond with a harsh word in return.

Don't misunderstand. There *is* a time and place for a raised voice, for turning up the volume control a notch. A child who refuses to listen or lazily tunes you out may need an earful of louder-than-usual advice. God made quite a noise from time to time to capture the attention of disobedient Israel, so it's not a surprise that we have to do the same. But this should be an exception, an attention grabber.

If you're in the habit of yelling, even your shouts can be tuned out. "There goes Dad again, yelling like a maniac. How red is his face today? Some day that blood vein on his forehead is going to pop!

What did he say, anyway?" If you're normally calm and in control, however, a rise in your tone will be a stand-at-attention shocker. It will cut through lazy ears like a chainsaw. Still, even on the waves of your louder voice, your words should never carry evil content or vengeful rhetoric. Tell the truth, speak your commands, and follow up your words with action.

As you carry out discipline with a tempered voice, remind your child of the consequences of his behavior, that he should not be surprised at receiving punishment that fits his crime. And always give him opportunity to respond.

When a conflict arises with my children, I follow a simple guideline regarding one-on-one discussions with them; they're free to express their feelings as long as they do so with calmness and respect. They can even tell me how awful they think I've been, complain about the bad decisions I've made, and I won't punish them for simply telling me what's on their minds. They know that if they maintain civility, they're free to tell me anything without fear of retribution of any kind. This discipline trains them to provide soft answers, to express their views without attacking anyone or otherwise losing control. And I've found that gentle discussions frequently invite open hearts, leading to deepening relationships and genuine understanding. This is a greater goal than a simple cease-fire; it is true fellowship that expands understanding and trust for both father and child.

Be careful not to limit conversations like this to times of discipline. Make a habit of trying to start conversations, even if your teenagers tend to grunt in reply. Your openness will be an everlasting sign of approachability, a wide-open path to your mind. Many wars can be avoided through negotiation, and if you can keep the communication lines in working order, you'll foster an environment of peace. In other words, let your kids know that when they call, they'll never get a busy signal.

Fathers, some of you have children who are in deep rebellion, and you may wonder how this method will work for you. How can you respond peacefully when a child is vengeful and destructive not only to others but to himself as well? The answer is, once again, overcome evil with good. If you ever stoop to the level of answering evil with evil, then the child has no reason to return to God, for you have shown him that your faith is not strong enough to keep you in peace. What good is Christianity if it doesn't work for you? At the end of the day, it's your faithfulness that will bring him home, not harsh rhetoric. It's the unconditional love you display that will shine forth as he experiences the false love of the world. Yes, you can use a "tough love" approach, if appropriate, but never with revenge or malice in your heart. Unrighteous anger is almost impossible to hide, and it will drive a prodigal son or daughter even farther away.

The bottom line is, whatever the situation, no matter how horrible an attack we experience in our homes, we can try to overcome evil with good. While it is true that not all conflicts can be avoided this way, wars on the home front cannot last long when one of the parties refuses to answer evil in kind.

## *Peace among Your Children*

Even if we already have a relatively peaceful environment at home, no matter how hard we try to avoid it, there's a daily potential for conflict. No two people are alike. We have preferences that differ from one another. Brother loves to whistle his favorite tunes; sister clamps her hands over her ears, moaning in pain. Dad likes the house to feel like Siberia; Mom prefers the Sahara.

It would be impossible to provide solutions to every nitpicky problem that arises among siblings. We can establish guidelines, however, though even these may seem inadequate when sisters quarrel and brothers come to blows. There is one overriding theme, however, in almost any conflict: both children, both parties in the battle, are demonstrating a lack of love. One might be the more self-ish of the two, to be sure, but the other has also not sacrificed his rights. One may have begun the war, but the other has struck back, violating the principle of overcoming evil with good.

After I break up a conflict, I describe the selfish behavior of both offenders focusing most of my displeasure on the one who fired the first shot. I then distribute discipline based on my estimation of guilt and age-appropriateness. In order to avoid future conflict, I remind the one who merely responded to the first volley to overcome evil with good or at least to walk away and report misbehavior to Mom or Dad.

Since I also don't want to create a tongue-wagging tattler, I tell my children to report only the following violations: (1) behavior that might bring harm to the perpetrator or to others, including any act of physical violence, (2) destruction of property, or (3) direct defi-ance of a parental rule. Squabbles over fairness, petty "I had it first" complaints, and other minor irritants should be left to private nego-tiation. Yes, one child may take advantage of another, but I tell the disadvantaged child that God knows what's going on. I remind him that it would be best to sacrifice his rights, show an attitude of love and servanthood, and let God take care of the offending sibling.

Peace among your children is founded in love, in sacrificial will-ingness to ignore the pain of the first blow, overcoming it with kind words and thoughtful deeds. As we teach our children to model the gospel in this way, they will learn to be like Christ, Who willingly bore our sins and gave us heaven in return for nails and thorns.

## ✧ Peace outside the Home

For the whole Law is fulfilled in one word, in the statement, "You shall love your neighbor as yourself." But if you bite and devour

one another, take care lest you be consumed by one another.
(Gal. 5:14, 15)

In most of the conflict examples in the previous chapter, there
existed an option to call for peace, the entreaty step that precedes
warfare. As sons of God, we're to be peacemakers (see Matt. 5:9),
using entreaty to avoid the horrors of war. We should always seek to
preserve peace when we're affronted, even if we believe our efforts
will ultimately fail. Even in the stormy midst of secular affairs, when
we're faced with strident people who have no love for God or His
precepts, the principle of overcoming evil with good can soothe the
most savage opponent.

To love your neighbor is to give graciously in sacrificial service.
It's practically impossible for someone to maintain hatred and
aggression if you're constantly loving and giving. As fathers, we're to
lead the charge of love outside of our homes, demonstrating the
spirit of Christ, who was oppressed and afflicted, yet did not open
His mouth (see Isa. 53:7).

## A Shaggy Dog Story

I thought a war might be brewing when a trio of my neighbor's dogs
took issue with my jogging path one day. As I passed in front of their
home, they ran out of their yard and onto the road, encircling me,
barking and lunging. After dodging and kicking them to avoid being
bitten, I finally ran far enough down the street to get out of range of
their protective instincts. I could have called Animal Control right
away and had the unruly beasts taken away, but since they had only
bothered me, and not one of my children, I felt it best to allow the
inconvenience and turn the other cheek.

That same day, however, my wife, Susie, and three of our daughters toured the neighborhood on bicycles, and one of the girls rode
ahead and out of Susie's sight. My daughter reported that these same

dogs ran after her, nipping at her heels. I shudder to think what might have happened if she had fallen. Upon hearing that story, I felt the urge to go to war. The safety of my children was at stake. I was prepared to do whatever was necessary, even destroying the dogs, to protect my girls.

Again, I could have called Animal Control immediately, but as I prescribed in the previous chapter, I first took the step of entreaty. Taking along one of my sons, I visited my neighbor. I thought my son's presence important for two reasons: 1) to teach him how to confront a situation in peace, and 2) to display a peaceful approach for the sake of my neighbor. Having a youngster around seems to promote a nonaggressive environment. Strangely enough, the dogs didn't seem to mind our entry into the yard. Their owner wasn't home, but the woman we spoke to promised to deliver our request to keep the dogs under control.

The next day, my daughter, Amanda, and I went for a walk, taking our dog along on a leash. As we passed by our neighbor's property, we noticed that one of their goats had become caught in the fence, her horns wedged so tightly she would never get out on her own. We tried to free her, but we didn't have enough strong hands to hold the fence, push the goat's head through, and keep our dog from lunging at the struggling goat at the same time. We decided to pay our neighbor another visit and tell her about the poor nanny.

As we approached, the three dogs went nuts, and their owner came out, yelling for us to leave, blaming our dog's presence for her dogs' behavior. I motioned for Amanda to hurry away with our dog and then calmly explained that we were there to tell her about her goat's dilemma. The woman immediately calmed down, and we had a pleasant conversation about her dogs, her goats, and life in general. She promised to keep her gates closed to prevent her dogs from wandering out of the yard, and we parted in peace.

Our neighbor had already heard my complaint about her dogs, so when we walked into her yard, literally armed to the teeth with our own dog, she probably expected conflict. Our efforts to do a good deed and our calm demeanor brought peace. In this case, we were not yet battling an evil enemy. We avoided a conflict by carrying an offering of peace. We overcame an intense attitude with good.

## Be at Peace with All People

This great biblical concept applies in every walk of life. If you have a border war with your neighbor, invite him to dinner and then walk around your yard to talk it out. If your coworker accuses you of backstabbing, ask him to go to a ball game with you and then out for pizza to poke at pepperonis while you hash through the conflict. If a government official abuses your rights, call him, and with your most pleasant voice, ask for an arbitrator. All of these fulfill Paul's command, "But if your enemy is hungry, feed him, and if he is thirsty, give him a drink" (Rom. 12:20), and after the burning coals of perplexity do their work, you may succeed in making an enemy into a friend.

I'm sure we can all think of a dozen more possibilities that might create conflict outside of our homes, but each one can be approached with the same principle. We should simply ask, "How can I make entreaty for peace? How can I overcome evil, or imminent conflict, with good deeds and sacrificial acts of kindness?" As we train our minds to respond in this manner, we can eliminate rash retorts and harsh words, imitating God, the ultimate peacemaker.

Fathers, I encourage you to include your children in your peacemaking efforts whenever it's appropriate. Learning about God's peace-loving ways is best accomplished through your example. Don't be shy about shining your light for them to see. Tell them exactly what you're doing and why. To them, you might just be Magnus the Great, and the image of the strongest man in the world bowing his head in sacrifice may be the most memorable monument to peace they'll ever see.

## ✦ Summary

Overcome evil with good. This is the foundation for peace. It takes a powerful man to withhold his sword, to refrain from a natural desire to give an evil man what he deserves. It takes a man of faith to trust God to execute perfect justice.

We strive for peace through sacrifice, giving up retribution and replacing it with good deeds. Swords and arrows have never converted a single soul, but soft answers make soft hearts as they bring into an aggressor's mind a new law, one that violates "an eye for an eye."

This principle works inside the home, and it begins with peace between husband and wife. Displaying true spousal unity is the family foundation, the rock upon which our children stand. Conflict between husband and wife will destroy a home, shaking it at its core. Fathers can avoid this catastrophe in two ways: by never beginning a battle and by never responding to an attack in a negative or hurtful way.

Peace with our children follows the same principle. Although we may have to raise our voices to gain attention, this should be rare, and our communication should never carry spiteful or vengeful words. Keep the lines of communication open, allowing your children to speak freely, even if they have unreasonable complaints. As long as they maintain civility, they should be allowed to share whatever is on their minds without fear of punishment.

Maintaining peace among our children is sometimes a monumental task. Since they don't seem to pop out of the same mold, children have a huge assortment of likes and dislikes and a great range of temperaments. As we teach them the art of sacrifice in the face of unfairness, they'll learn to be like Christ, ushering in peace instead of answering in kind and fostering war.

Carrying the principle of overcoming evil with good to the outside world reflects God's love for everyone. There's almost always room for entreaty, and giving our enemies the opportunity to cease hostilities allows them to follow the path of peace. If we go to war with them, we'll have given them up to evil. Yes, war may be necessary, but it is not ideal.

As we share peace with the world, our children can learn as they observe how we practically apply God's design in day-to-day life. We should take them along to the scene of impending conflict whenever we can, so they can see both the act and the attitude of loving sacrifice, how it really can change hearts. That way, as they see God working, their faith can be increased, and their love for others can be established. And fathers, this is the gospel in action.

# The Father as Husband

##  The Perfect Standard

> For your husband is your Maker,
> Whose name is the Lord of hosts;
> And your Redeemer is the Holy One of Israel,
> Who is called the God of all the earth. (Isa. 54:5)

It's hard for me to think of God as my husband. Although I'm not into being a super macho kind of guy, I do enjoy traditionally masculine pursuits, and thinking about being someone's bride doesn't exactly fit my idea of feeling manly. When I meditate on God's husband-like qualities, however, I begin to understand the reasons He describes Himself as the husband of His people and why He sees the church as His bride.

As a father, it's important to learn these attributes of God and how to display them, giving your wife the same kind of sacrificial, loving provision Christ gives to the church. Even if you're not married, or you and your wife are separated, you can still model some of these loving aspects of God's husband heart. As you joyfully imitate Jesus, your children will not only learn more about their Savior, but they will also watch you paint a portrait of a husband.

A son, a husband in training, will watch you as though looking in the mirror at his future self, guiding, protecting, and providing for a soul mate. He won't have to seek a bride in ignorance of his own role as a suitor. As a man who has learned what a husband ought to be, your son will be able to attract a woman who expects to be treated like the bride of Christ, a lady of purity who will gladly be in subjection to her man's leadership as the church is to its Savior.

A daughter will see in your face the image of another man, the one waiting at the end of the wedding aisle, the one to whom you will present her as a spotless bride (see 2 Cor. 11:2). How will she learn what kind of character to expect from a godly husband if not from you? And as suitors make their case, she'll be able to filter their qualities through a grid of firmly established principles, the measure of her righteous Shepherd.

As we outline a few of these qualities, we'll see how our children imitate our actions as we diligently follow the model God has set before us, the standard of the perfect husband.

## ✧ A Husband Sacrifices

Jesus established a relationship with His people through sacrifice. Without His death there could be no fellowship with Him, no purging of our separating barrier, no cleansing from sin. He is the bridegroom who went to war to free His bride from slavery, willingly laying down His life to set her free.

Sacrifice is the foundation of a husband's relationship with his wife. Sacrifice begins at the altar with a vow of complete fidelity. Sacrifice continues every dawn as a husband greets the rising sun with a prayer on his lips for his wife's protection, a plan in his mind for her well-being, and a Bible in his hands for her nourishment. Sacrifice never ends until a husband draws his last breath and whispers a blessing to his wife before he commits his spirit to God. Sacrifice dominates and permeates every day of married commitment. Actions embrace words, and our hands and feet move to spell out love.

God has shown us in the three persons of the Trinity the breadth of His sacrificial love, a triangle of giving that never ends. As we look at these marvelous gifts from God, we'll learn how to imitate His ways, teaching each aspect to our children as they watch our model of God's grace grow into the likeness of Christ Himself.

## God the Sacrificer

> For what the Law could not do, weak as it was through the flesh, God did: sending His own Son in the likeness of sinful flesh and as an offering for sin, He condemned sin in the flesh. (Rom. 8:3)

God our Father made the ultimate sacrifice, sending His only Son as an offering for sin. As a model of God on earth, a husband is willing to sacrifice everything he holds dear—his life, his health, and his freedom.

I say "freedom" because, while some men will endure pain and risk personal harm for the sake of their wives, they may not want to give up their off-duty time. In other words, when the whistle blows at five o'clock, they punch their time cards and head for the television, the newspaper, the computer, or a book and insist on having this personal time to unwind. They want the freedom to be a part-time husband and father.

While it's true that you may need a break to recharge, don't insist on taking even an hour to open a can of selfishness; it's poison to your soul. Even if you sit to get a moment's rest, try to view interruptions to your repose as another opportunity to serve God, not as irritating intrusions into your personal time. You're not a part-time husband, nor are you a hireling in the field of fathering. There's no hour of self-indulgence. Every moment is given to God and, through your vows, given to your wife.

You may have treasured activities, favorite hobbies or sports diversions, but you should always have twine and torch on hand to tie them up and burn them on the sacrificial altar should they ever interfere with time and energy that might be spent on your beloved bride.

Years ago, I played computer games for my own enjoyment. They can be a relaxing distraction, a way to recharge. But one day the wastefulness of that time struck me. Here I was, just sitting in front of an impersonal screen. What benefit was anyone deriving from my leisure? I found that time spent with my children, interacting and playing games with them, was not only more relaxing, it also edified them. When put in perspective, the sacrifice was easily made, because love drove me to hang that indulgence on the cross.

If God could make the ultimate sacrifice for rebellious sinners (see Rom. 5:8), how much more should we be able to offer everything for our soul mates, the ladies God gave us to nourish and cherish? How can we not give our all for our children, the little lambs in our beloved flock? In an atmosphere of love, sacrifice becomes joy, a shout of gladness. And each sacrificial act strengthens us to give even more. Such is the heart of our loving God.

## God the Servant

Have this attitude in yourselves which was also in Christ Jesus, who, although He existed in the form of God, did not regard equality with God a thing to be grasped, but emptied Himself, taking the form of a bond-servant, and being made in the likeness of men. And being found in appearance as a man, He humbled Himself by becoming obedient to the point of death, even death on a cross. (Phil. 2:5–8)

God the Son established Himself as a servant. He could have asserted His authority as the Lord of all, taking a throne and having people grovel at His feet. He chose instead to kneel with a towel and wash their dirty feet. Although Jesus led His disciples, teaching them and commanding them as a shepherd tends his sheep, He also protected and rescued them, snatching one from the swallowing sea, guarding others from its smashing waves, and walking on its foamy steps to lead His people out of seas of danger. Even as a multitude hailed Him as the triumphant ruler, He prepared Himself as the ultimate sacrifice. While crossing a carpet of palms in the midst of a wave of kisses and cries of "Hosanna!" He knew He would soon climb a rocky path through a wave of spittle and shouts of "Crucify Him!"

How do you imitate such a sacrificial model? Look for opportunities to serve every moment of the day, especially in areas too burdensome for others. You were given a strong back and broad shoulders for good reason, so your weaker vessel can look to you to bear heavy burdens, whether physical or spiritual.

I frequently tell Susie, "Don't worry about that. I'll take care of it." With those words the shadows of anxiety flee away. She may give me a list of phone calls she's not comfortable making, and once the list is on my desk, she can wipe the issues from her slate of worries. She doesn't concern herself with income taxes, home security, or our next Bible lesson. This is my service to our family, and she knows it well.

Even in jobs your wife can normally accomplish, you can still be of service. Are the dishes done? Is she carrying a heavy load? Does the toilet paper need changing? How about the light bulbs? And you should never ask, "Whose turn is it to change the diaper?" In your mind it should be your turn, no matter how messy it is. No, you won't have to change it every time; that's not the point. It's the attitude of your mind. Your heart seeks to serve; it doesn't search for a way out.

As a young father, one statement I kept quoting to myself helped me immensely: "I can always wash my hands." It seems that the most helpful forms of servanthood require the messiest activities. From infant fecal explosions to greasy cooking messes to head-lice treatments, getting my hands covered with something awful is a requirement for duty. When the last tape is pressed on the Pampers, when the bottom of the grease trap is reached, when the final nit is picked, then I can pause to wash my hands. Each stain reminds me of service, and washing foretells my next act of service, preparing me once again to give up my rights to comfort and clean hands.

After the nails, after the thorns, the blood of Christ set its stains. Holy hands carried its cleansing flood to my soul. How evil were my ways! How filthy was my sin! Yet Jesus loved me enough to get His hands dirty. He was raised, He was glorified, and even now He guides my way, His cleansed hand leading mine down dangerous paths, my Shepherd still coming to my aid.

## God the Helper

> And I will ask the Father, and He will give you another Helper, that He may be with you forever; that is the Spirit of truth, whom the world cannot receive, because it does not behold Him or know Him, but you know Him because He abides with you, and will be in you. (John 14:16, 17)

God, in the person of the Holy Spirit, has come as our helper (verse 16). Even as Christ came to do what was impossible for us, the Holy Spirit comes to help us do the possible. In other words, Christ set us free from bonds we could not cut; the Holy Spirit helps us to serve as freed men and women in Christ. With His empowering presence, we can do all things He has called us to do (see Phil. 4:13). He teaches us, bringing God's Word to our minds. He comes alongside to help us obey, reminding us of God's commands and showing us how to escape temptation. He lights our path, allowing us to anticipate the future as we listen to His voice of discernment.

It is true that a woman's work is never done. After she moves one mountain, there always seems to be another one right behind it, taller, wider, and heavier than the first. Still she rolls up her sleeves and plugs away. She has her own model, the woman portrayed in Proverbs 31, the lady who had it all together. And hers is a high calling, carrying burdens no man was designed to lift.

Does she complain? Does she give up in frustration? With tufts of her own hair in her hands, does she thrust a squirming toddler into your arms and run out the front door screaming?

If you don't model the Holy Spirit's helping ways, she just might. As Proverbs 31 teaches, a godly woman can work wonders, but without a helper even she would find insanity a possible option. With help from her husband, however, a wife feels energized to move a dozen mountains, because her life mate cares enough to come alongside and push his shovel in next to hers.

I can tell when my wife, Susie, needs a boost; I hear gentle sighs and I see her head slowly shaking. As the primary teacher in our home school, she has enormous responsibilities, and each teaching day is a mountain of assignments, corrections, reports, tests, crafts, field trips, lesson plans, and frustration. She goes to bed exhausted only to wake up to a fresh new mountain of assignments, corrections, reports, tests, crafts, field trips, lesson plans, and even more frustration. Though our home school is usually a place of joy, once in a while a huge pile of accumulated labors can weigh her down.

When I hear those sighs, I know it's time to lend a hand. I already share in the teaching duties on a daily basis, but now and then I take a heavier load, checking papers, helping with crafts, and dreaming up ideas for projects. Just knowing that I'm pitching in can swing her mood. She feels her teammate at her side, not only leading the cheers, but also lending a listening ear, offering advice when requested, and, most of all, mixing his sweat with hers.

A willing helper energizes and encourages, bringing hope to any woman who has to overcome a mountain of labors. Too much work frustrates and slows, but staring hopelessly at an unscalable mountain demoralizes and immobilizes. When her husband arrives with a plan of attack and a lively mood, he brings new vigor and renewed commitment. As you model the energizing Holy Spirit, look for opportunities to come alongside your long-suffering mate. You'll be amazed at how quickly the sighs turn into smiles.

We fathers, even those who have no wives, can imitate the sacrificial ways of our Lord, the perfect husband model. We have the authority to command and the responsibility to teach, carrying out our duty as shepherds of whomever God has given us to lead. Yet, in our leadership, if we demonstrate the act of daily dying to self, we will accomplish our goal of imitating Christ who gave His life for us. In sacrifice, in service, in helps, we show the image of our triune God in all His manifestations, One who loves with actions that match His words.

## ✧ A Husband Defends

The Lord is my light and my salvation;
Whom shall I fear?
The Lord is the defense of my life;
Whom shall I dread? (Ps. 27:1)

The songs of King David are filled with celebrations of God's defending shield. With God at his side, David had no fear, for his ever-present protector had never failed him. He remembered God's commandments, and he trusted God's promises. David knew that God's word was never empty; his Lord always filled a promise with faithful action.

God has a design for marriage, a design He set in place at the dawn of creation. Adam and Eve were cleaved into one flesh for a twofold purpose—Eve as a helpmate to Adam, and Adam as her provider-protector. Together, they were a unit, fulfilling each other's needs in mutual sacrifice. Separated, they became vulnerable, Eve to attack from their great enemy, Adam to temptation from his wife who, once abandoning her role as helpmate, became his seductress, a role Adam could not have expected.

Although Eve was the first to sin, Adam, to be sure, was also guilty. He was warned, and he had no excuse. The point is that the first couple's separation made both individuals weaker. As a result, both Adam and Eve fell, snared by neglecting a built-in strength—unity—that Satan seemed to know very well.

Satan was the first to use the divide and conquer strategy, and he still employs it today. It's not, however, simple physical separation that most often breaks down the unity of husband and wife. It's a division in spirit that brings the greatest harm and drives a wedge in the union that no man can put asunder.

I grieve when I hear husbands and wives talking negatively about each other. Whether in jest or in earnest, they cut each other down, sometimes laughing after their little digs bite like razor teeth through the emotional skin of their mates. "Oh, it's not so bad," they say. "We were just joking." Yet unseen blood pours from their wounds, building a sea of separation.

My worst memories of this heartbreaking activity come from a church Valentine's dinner, of all places. We played a game in which we took the letters in "valentine" and wrote a list of our spouses' qualities, each beginning with one of the letters. I expected to hear words of kindness, husbands and wives testifying to the world of their undying devotion to each other. Instead, I heard deeply cutting remarks, each one followed by an obligatory laugh. "V is for vacant," she begins, "his mind when he watches football." "A is for airhead," he retorts, "my wife when she's driving." With each hurtful word, I saw couples literally moving farther apart, their laughs filling the room like fairy tales—pretty, sweet, and easy—but nobody really believing they reflected the truth. I had two opportunities to use a letter, and with both I offered glowing descriptions of my wonderful wife, Susie. A few couples approved; many others seemed angry. Such is the typical response when a light is cast upon sin.

I will never publicly speak a negative word about Susie. If I have a problem with something she has said or done, I will speak to her alone. In fact, both alone and publicly, I will edify her with generous compliments, whether she's there to hear them or not. My words compose a garland, decorating her with wreaths of love, letting everyone know what an angelic saint she really is. I bear witness to my children that I adore her, that I would rather die than allow one drop of her blood to spill, either physically or emotionally, because of my lack of defense.

As the evil one knows, when a husband and wife are separated by words or by emotional or physical space, they're the most vulnerable. Hurtful words create an emotional separation, while living in different worlds creates a dangerous chasm. If a wife enters the workplace, she's especially prone to attack from the serpent's fellows dangling modern forbidden fruit. She leaves the world of her home, the sphere of protection and influence created by her husband, and blends into a new cosmos that competes for her loyalty and devotion.

Her husband takes great risk to allow her to enter such a valley of darkness without his protective shield, and the fruits of sin gathered by her hand and brought back to the home have shattered many marriages. It would take an entire book to describe the kinds of temptations that arise and the steps to destruction each one can cause a person to take, but the basic principle is fairly simple. A wife was designed by God to be her husband's helpmate. If she physically separates herself from him and goes to be the helpmate of another, she leaves his sphere of influence and authority and risks emotional separation. Her loyalties become divided. Her husband cannot see or defend against the temptations, and she may return a changed person. Who knows what poison she might bring home, even unaware?

As a defending husband, you give your wife security. She will never fear the possibility of unfaithfulness; she will never doubt your loyalty. There is no fear or dread in the mind of a warrior's wife. Your defending actions, both in word and deed, prove to her that you're trustworthy. As your children watch you surround her with shields of protection and decorate her with wreaths of love, they'll learn how a husband ought to value his woman, and they'll see an image of how Christ loves His church.

## ✧ A Husband Teaches

The Scriptures tell us directly that the Holy Spirit is a teacher, and as a husband, you act in the same capacity for your wife. Yes, she also possesses the same Spirit, but God has given you the responsibility to carry out part of His duty, to be a spiritual guide for her and your children, a leader and motivator for pursuing spiritual and intellectual wisdom and knowledge. We covered the role of teacher in chapter 4, so we'll not retrace the lesson here. We do need to remind ourselves, however, that as we guide our wives, we're modeling yet another aspect of God—the husband—and allowing our children to see this aspect of fatherhood in action.

## ✧ A Husband Loves

> I want you to swear, O daughters of Jerusalem,
> Do not arouse or awaken my love,
> Until she pleases. (Song of Sol. 8:4)

The Song of Solomon is the classic expression of a married couple's affection for each other. It's filled with poetic imagery, showing us the romantic vision of one lover in the eyes of another. Solomon's lady is beautiful in form, in fragrance, and in elegance. He treats her as a treasured jewel, not even allowing anyone to wake her should she wish to slumber. Such is his unselfish devotion.

Shall you not also sing that song? No matter how anyone else views your wife, in your eyes she's the most beautiful woman in the world. You see her love, her inner strength, her faithfulness. What kind of song will you sing for her?

When you show passionate affection, you tell another truth about Jesus and His church. Yours is not just a ceremonial commitment to the "I do's" of your matrimonial vows. You're not married to the law of the marriage covenant; you're cleaved to a person, a woman with emotions, dreams, and desires. And as a child of God, you do not follow the Lord according to a codified set of rules, a rigid collection of "Thou shalt not's." Your relationship with Christ is personal, deep, probing, satisfying. In many ways, you are married to Him.

The first and most obvious way you can demonstrate your abiding love is to show real affection. Your children need to see more than the requisite "love peck" kisses to believe there's more to your passion than what is obligated by law. And if you playact with false displays, they'll be able to see through the façade. Your interaction needs to reflect truth; it needs to be a visible image of your invisible union.

My children would think something's wrong if I were to pass by Susie more than a couple of times without a touch or a hug. Even after more than twenty years of bliss, I take her in my arms several times a day and embrace her tenderly, passing the warmth of my delight in her from body to body. It is not duty; it is zeal. Every time I see her, I want to sing with Solomon, "Arise my darling, my beautiful one, and come with me" (2:13). And I want her to feel my joy as she sings in reply, "He has brought me to his banquet hall, and his banner over me is love!" (2:4).

Our union with Christ is invisible, an abiding wedlock that no one else can see. Yet, He calls us to display that relationship for everyone, as He said, "By this all men will know that you are My disciples, if you have love for one another." It is our visible expressions of love that communicate our passion, that reveal our underlying motivations to glorify and honor the one whom we love—wife, brother, sister, and ultimately Jesus Christ. We show God's love to the world with our words and deeds, revealing the love we have for the brothers and sisters in whom Christ dwells.

In the movie, *Fiddler on the Roof*, Tevye sings to Golda, his wife, "Do You Love Me?" a song that begs for the lovely words of affection to come from her lips. She replies that she has shown her love through her service, "For twenty-five years I've washed your clothes, cooked your meals, cleaned your house, given you children, milked your cows." She concludes, "If that's not love, what is?" Then, in a touching finale, her emotions wrap around her realization that she really loves her husband. Sitting close together they sing, "It doesn't change a thing, but after twenty-five years, it's nice to know."

Yes, it's nice to know. With our words singing in harmony with our deeds, our love flows visibly, and every aspect of married affection resounds, letting everyone know that the union of two into one, God's invisible cleaving miracle, is indeed for real.

Our love is not spelled out in words alone, nor is it manifested only in deeds. It is also sanctified and made perfect in absolute faithfulness, a sign to the world that a husband's fidelity with his wife is parallel to God's with His people. Just as God forgives and redeems no soul outside of faith in Jesus Christ, so a man takes no woman into his bed or his heart except for his wife, the one with whom he has made a covenant of faith.

A man should not only refrain from touching another woman in a sensual way, he should not even entertain the notion with his thoughts or words. Some may think flirting harmless, but playful words tell a woman that your heart is divided; they let everyone around know that you wish to play games of infidelity in your mind. This man has a wandering heart. His heart is not completely fused to his wife's; it seeks other pleasures.

Being above reproach, carefully guarding your witness to faithfulness, extends to appearances as well. If you're alone with another woman, even if all your thoughts and activities are perfectly pure, the spatial union may cause problems. Any witness may assume that you desire this time alone with her, that you may be pursuing activities that violate your vows.

Who cares what others think? God does. As Paul wrote, "that you may prove yourselves to be blameless and innocent, children of God above reproach in the midst of a crooked and perverse generation, among whom you appear as lights in the world" (Phil. 2:15). If you find yourself alone with a female who is not your wife or daughter, seek a more public place to carry out your business. Leave the door open or move outside. Call someone else into the room. Do whatever is necessary to bear witness to the wholesomeness of your activities.

Why should you take such precautions? As Paul wrote, this is a crooked and perverse generation, and sinful people will project their sinfulness onto you. Since they're corrupt, they'll assume that you're no better. If you always seek to keep your activities open and in the light, you will not allow an avenue of attack; you will never cast God's faithfulness in a bad light.

As you display such dedication to your vow of faithfulness in all your actions, you paint a beautiful portrait for your children.

They'll see a husband who has a single-minded purpose—to bring love, joy, peace, and salvation to his wife, the one and only woman in his heart. That portrait, the image of a faithful man, will become for them a window to the heart of God. Through you they will see God's unwavering fidelity, the promise of His covenantal love.

What better way to introduce our little ones to God? From the time they can understand the symbol of our intertwined hands to the day one of us sings a funeral farewell to the other, our children will view the bond they should have with God. Our song begins with hands matching our hearts, intertwined by covenant and by choice, and it ends on earth with hearts forever joined, though one hand must leave the other for a short while. Let our children forever hear that song! It will resound in their minds as they search for a lover who will fulfill our lyrics, and it will soften their hearts to receive the everlasting love of God.

## Take Root in Me

Take root in me
And cast aside all doubt and fear
Of seeds that die and fail to thrive.
What God hath sown in fertile ground
Will bear our fruit a hundred fold
And fill the world with gospel sound.

Take root in me
In soil prepared for my beloved
With holy water sprinkled pure.
Tilled straight to bury deep His Word
We'll burst anew in fragrant psalms
In seasons fresh till all have heard.

Take root in me
And make me strong in thy embrace;
Forbid that I should anchor not.
Without thy roots there is no hold;
Erosion's tides would wash away
And leave me barren, pale, and cold.

Take root in me
To hold you up and feed thy growth
Surrounded by my warm caress.
You'll be my lover, fair with grace,
A rose, a blossom, wisdom's head,
The crown of glory there to place.

Take root in me
This body give I all to thee
'Tis all I have save only this,
The soul which God hath claimed his own.
But it will catch a hand of yours
And take it to our final home.

—BRYAN DAVIS

## ✧ Summary

As the bridegroom rejoices over the bride, so your God will rejoice over you. (Isa. 62:5)

A crucial aspect of fatherhood involves showing our children the husband-like qualities of God—His devotion, His faithfulness, and His protection. A son will look to his father to demonstrate what a husband is, what a husband does. A daughter sees in Daddy the image of a future mate, learning how she ought to be treated by a man who will someday sweep her away.

A husband is first a sacrificial servant. As Christ gave His all for His bride, the church, so should a man lay down every aspect of his life for his wife. God shows us His sacrificial love in three major ways, each represented in one of the persons of the trinity.

God the Father gave His only Son as the ultimate sacrifice, and we should be willing to give up anything of value that would interfere with providing for our wives. God the Son walked the earth as a servant, and we walk in His footsteps, bringing our strong helping hands to bear any load. God the Holy Spirit is our abiding helper, our example of coming alongside to aid our wives, even in tasks they could do themselves. In a sense, we parallel the ministry of the Holy Spirit, energizing and enabling our wives.

A husband also acts as his wife's chief defender. He's programmed to protect his wife from anyone who might do her harm. If they're separated, either by physical or emotional space, she is vulnerable to attack. A husband's words can drive an emotional wedge or apply a spiritual bond. He must pledge to choke on any word that might cut her down and thereby cut into their bonding fiber. His speech should rather be like honey, not false, not saccharin, only the true expression of his undying love for her.

A husband is a lover, a man who attaches to his wife's inner person, interacting with her mind and all its dreams and desires. He doesn't simply do his duty as a husband; he shows real affection, giving her tactile symbols of his emotional attachment. Whether with hugs, terms of endearment, or flowery poetry, he communicates his inner union with her mind in ways she can understand. He also demonstrates his love through his commitment to absolute fidelity, both in mind and in body. His covenant parallels Christ's covenant with His bride, those who come to Him by faith.

CHAPTER

12

# The Father as Counselor

## ✧ The Song Begins

> When my heart was embittered,
> And I was pierced within,
> Then I was senseless and ignorant;
> I was like a beast before Thee.
> Nevertheless I am continually with Thee;
> Thou hast taken hold of my right hand.
> With Thy counsel Thou wilt guide me,
> And afterward receive me to glory. (Ps. 73:21–24)

A solitary water oak stands in my backyard. Its ball-shaped field of branches creates a haven for birds, a thick web of leaves allowing in filtered sunlight to warm their feathers while hiding their plans for the future. A nest slowly takes shape. When the last strand of horsehair is threaded in place, the male flits to the highest perch and chirps about his coming brood while his mate settles into the nest's protective pocket. I listen to his song, the familiar melody of a proud father, and I know his heart.

Days later, three turquoise eggs appear, barely an inch long and splotched with coffee-like stains. Hope reigns. Love and warmth radiate to growing embryos until they spring forth, featherless freaks with wide-open mouths. Mother and father provide. Babies grow. Feathers sprout and wings unfurl. Wobbly legs step to the precipice, and with tiny flaps the nestlings leap into the outside world, leaving the water oak's protective shield.

I see the empty nest. Mother and Father mockingbird are nowhere to be seen. Just last week, one or both would have dive-bombed my head, shrieking and swooping in dire warning. Today, all is quiet. The home is abandoned, and only its memories remain.

## ✧ The Arrows of Fortune

> Like arrows in the hand of a warrior,
> So are the children of one's youth.
> How blessed is the man whose quiver is full of them;
> They shall not be ashamed,
> When they speak with their enemies in the gate. (Ps. 127:4, 5)

What is an empty nest? Is it a symbol of sadness? Is it a monument to a legacy? Someday our children will leave the shelter of our homes, and their departure will create dramatic change. As the psalmist tells us, children are like arrows, and a warrior is blessed if his quiver is full of them. But what becomes of the warrior when the last arrow is taken from his quiver? What are his duties when his little warriors have gone forth and he's too old to march in their wars? In the book of our lives, careful attention to our role in this new phase will help us write a satisfying final chapter on fatherhood.

God equips us for service, and He sends us out to expand His kingdom, making spiritual war with anyone who would stand in His way. We are God's arrows, fitted for use by the ultimate warrior. Once He sends us out, He remains steady, true, and available, ready to guide our paths as we soar toward our targets.

When our children leave home to pursue their visions, they'll still need their father. Our role changes from one who asserts himself as a child's authority to one who moves into the background as a counselor. If a father has instilled godly wisdom in his children over the years, he sits in quiet confidence that they will find the right way, and he stays ready to assist them as they seek to interpret their circumstances in light of what they have learned.

We'll look at our preparation to send our children out into the world by analyzing the warrior illustration. Fathers, like God, are warriors, and our children are arrows. Every arrow has a special use, but each one is prepared according to similar principles. A father is well advised to learn the principles of good arrow making so he can be sure his are ready to fire.

Carrying any illustration too far causes it to break down. Obviously we can't guide an arrow once it leaves the string, and it can't come back for refiring unless we go out and retrieve it. We will, however, belabor the illustration for our purposes, hoping we don't stretch the bowstring beyond its breaking point.

After that, we'll look at what happens after our children leave, how we act as counselors from afar, consultants who are called upon when needed.

## A Straight Arrow

An arrow that can't fly straight is worthless. It takes off in the direction of the point, but with numerous bends and angles in the arrow shaft, who knows where it will finally end up? Trying to aim it is a waste of time, and it may cause unintended damage.

A child who is crafted according to the Word of God walks in a straight path. He knows God's commandments and his responsibility to obey them. He carries them in his heart as a beloved letter from his Lord. He has learned how to recognize God's voice, enabling him to walk the path his Shepherd has set before him, as the Proverb says, "Let your eyes look directly ahead, and let your gaze be fixed straight in front of you. Watch the path of your feet, and all your ways will be established" (Prov. 4:25, 26).

Preparing a child to leave home is not just formalizing a good-bye, the giving of a blessing and a few dollars for the road; it is a painstaking craft, a years-long labor of love. You can't wait until the day of departure to straighten out a son or daughter who has a heart bent away from God. Making the arrow straight requires patient carving, painful whittling away of defects, and prudent examination. If the Word of God is not abiding in a child's heart, there will be no steering influence when he walks out your door. He'll be left to the winds of the world.

Is there any greater anguish than to see a child going astray, the one in whom you have invested so many years? Even in such tragedy, there is still hope. There is still a powerful, loving God in heaven. And you, Father, can still make a difference. We'll cover that hope and what you can do to help in the last section of this chapter.

## An Accurate Arrow

A straight arrow flies in an unfailing path; it will not bend to the left or to the right of its trajectory. But what good is an arrow if it plunges into the wrong target? Straight is good, but straight into a brick wall is pointless.

In chapter 8 we discussed helping a child gain a vision, a purpose for life. By gaining this vision, a child will leave home with an aim, confidently stepping out into the world with a clear view of where he's going. Without vision, he'll fly in a straight path toward oblivion.

Many children leave home without a target in mind. They may not have their career paths set or know what courses they want to take in college. They may seem to be floating in a void. While it is ideal for departing children to have well-focused goals, they can still have great success even if they have only a vague idea of where they're going. Whether missions or medicine, homemaking or haberdashery, a child's calling in life can become more firmly established after he leaves home. A general aim, however, is still crucial, and you can help that aim come into view.

Here is the universal target. No matter what floors they finally walk—the tiles of hospitals, the carpets of home, or the stones and sands of foreign missions—if your children are tracing the footsteps of Christ's love, they'll be walking in a path that God will approve. An arrow is well aimed if it's pointed at the heart. If a child learns that nothing is more important than reaching out to people with the compassionate hand of Jesus, he or she will find a godly mark.

Corner offices are nothing more than idols of position, military ranks are merely saluted ribbons and buttons, and government seats of power are the money-brokered thrones of the ambitious. Yet, even though Nicodemus wore the robe of the Pharisee, he sought the heart of Christ, yearning for the feet of his Savior more than for the seat of power. If you teach your children to love, to bleed for people as Christ bled for the nations, no matter where their feet tread, they *will* find God's path.

Our aim is to fulfill the calling of the gospel's work within us. God's love changes hearts; our children are called to take that transforming message to others, no matter which path will lead them to that end. If we aim for the heart, our arrows will not need to be retrieved and fired again.

## A Fast Arrow

An arrow that is straight and well aimed will strike its target, but what effect will it have? If it fails to pierce the surface and bounces off without even making a mark, the arrow has failed. It has flown with precision, but without the speed necessary to make an impact.

An arrow that strikes hard, that has an effect on the world, is sleek and sharp. Its shaft is lightweight, and its point is honed to a fine razor's edge. It strikes deep, and it carries out its mission.

This arrow is a child who is energetic and enthusiastic, not indulged or lazy. He's disciplined and self-motivated, carrying within his heart a burning desire to fulfill his vision. He doesn't carry the burdens of the world, because he's lifted up by faith, trusting in God to meet all his needs. He flies to his target with full confidence that God will prepare it beforehand, so that when he strikes, hearts will be ready to be transformed by the presence of one who carries the light of God's saving grace.

You can make these arrows by teaching your children discipline, by training them to love the benefits of exercise, both physical and spiritual. Do they love the Word of God, or is it a burden? Do they arise on their own in the morning, or do you have to roll them out of bed? Can they schedule and complete their assignments, or do you have to shadow them to make sure they do all their chores and homework?

Some children have a very hard time being self-motivated. With Mommy and Daddy in the house to cart them around, clean up after them, and monitor their "to do" checklists, they can turn into slugs who just slither from place to place, doing what they have to do simply to keep from being stepped on.

You don't want slugs in your house. Yes, help them set goals and priorities, but also teach inner reliance, allowing your children to fail and suffer the consequences of failure if necessary. If you prop them up and force success, success will not be their own; it will be surrogate, a poor substitute that will bring lazy hearts to any future effort.

Healthy children need no crutches; they need impetus, fire burning within. Light that fire through inspiration, not indulgence. Set an example and exhort them to follow your lead, to be imitators of you as you are of Christ (see 1 Cor. 11:1). That's how you make fast, hard-striking arrows. With hearts, minds, and bodies honed to sharp edges, they'll be ready to make a great impact on the world for Christ.

## An Enduring Arrow

In order to strike a target that's far away, an arrow has to be able to maintain its flight, cutting through wind and other elements without losing direction. A long flight requires that the warrior aim high, giving the arrow a trajectory that will follow a well-planned arc. Such an arrow is sculpted from hard wood, tacked with stiff feathering, and constructed with a well-balanced plan.

Sometimes life is difficult, and serving God requires weathering storms that buffet even straight, accurate arrows. In many pursuits, our children will learn to temper speed with patience, to pace themselves when their goals lie far in the future.

As counselors for our growing children, we know the value of endurance, the courage to go on even if trials arise. Having lived a few more years than they, we've come through long nights and we've seen the light of morning. We've viewed dark difficulties in hindsight, helping our patience and endurance to mature. Sitting in the well-lit perspective of the present time and pondering a trial from the safe platform of memory, we're able to take a deep breath and marvel at how God has guided us through shadowy days.

The shorter our years on earth, the longer a season of pain feels, making youthful suffering difficult to endure. Our children may not

have witnessed God's provision. They may not have been empowered to defeat a tenacious enemy or comforted after losing a battle
in a long war. That's why it's up to us to help our children learn how
to endure in their youthful struggles.

Although we should rescue them from immediate danger,
allowing them to struggle at times may bring lasting benefit, especially as we bring encouragement and reminders of how God has
helped us in the past. A child who is pulled out of every potential
snare will be weak, both in mind and body, unfit for the turmoil he
will surely face in the outside world.

Just as the chick must fight his way out of the egg to gain
strength for life, and just as a soldier must train his body in a controlled environment in order to face an unpredictable battle, so
should our children be trained in the safety of home, preparing them
for the shifting winds of the world.

There's an old adage that has helped me through many seasons of
storms. "What I have learned in the light, I will not doubt in the
dark." Through a number of difficult tests, I've learned that God really
does care about me, and with a spiritual branding iron, I emblazon
my mind with deep impressions of God's wonderful provisions.
Then, when the next test comes and pain sets in, I arouse those carefully stored memories and meditate on them, bringing soothing relief
and strength to go on. I have learned of God's love in the light of
day, and those memories will illumine even the darkest of nights.

Sharing memories like these will help your children endure.
They may not have a legacy of their own, a storehouse of past rescues from harm or comfort in times of trouble. Yet, they have a
resource, a library of sorts, your recollections of God's grace.
Spread them freely. Even if the stories seem to get old, they won't
be forgotten, and they will be a fresh breeze when they come to
mind during a season of distress.

Pressure hardens. Cold tightens. Dryness makes tough. Bitter herbs
make even coarse bread taste sweet. As the writer of Hebrews said,

"All discipline for the moment seems not to be joyful, but sorrowful; yet to those who have been trained by it, afterwards it yields the peaceful fruit of righteousness" (12:11). Unless our children are made into hardened arrows, they will not be ready to face the world.

Still, we want to maintain balance. Home is a place of comfort and joy as well as a training field. We don't want to unnaturally force difficult times on our children, but we do want them to endure through the everyday trials of life. And we should also require discipline in body and mind, plotting a course that seems natural, a way of life.

I require my older children to set their alarms and wake up on their own. They know when they're supposed to make their beds, exercise, come to morning devotions, and begin their schoolwork. They follow a reasonable schedule, not a boot camp regimen. Though we don't march them out to the scream of a drill sergeant, we do see to their compliance by doling out consequences for missing the mark. As the schedule becomes routine, it trains them to know no other way of life.

We hope our arrows carry that discipline to their own homes someday. We are aiming high, knowing that most goals worth gaining lie at the end of arduous journeys. May God help them see the light and remember its promises even during the lonely nights.

## A Familiar Arrow

> Now as they observed the confidence of Peter and John, and understood that they were uneducated and untrained men, they were marveling, and began to recognize them as having been with Jesus. (Acts 4:13)

When an arrow strikes its target, what will be its lasting impression? If it bears a symbol, an etching that reveals its sender, the people who discover it and realize its effect will honor the warrior, either with respect or fear.

As we send our children out, we hope their effect on the world will bring honor to the one who empowered them. Although some may wish to give credit to their parents, we hope to shift the glory to God, the source of all that is good. How can we put that etching on our children so all will know that Jesus is the true warrior who sent them out?

Those we affect can easily learn that God is our source. We tell them. Yet this is not as simple as it sounds. Jesus did not always reveal His true identity in a straightforward manner; He chose to be clear with some people and vague with others. As we teach our children to be like Christ when they leave our homes, we should remind them to reveal themselves as Christians both in stealth and in clarity, depending on their targets.

Their character will always mark them as Christians. Their unusual integrity in all matters will be strikingly new and odd to most. Those who know the mark of Christ will immediately recognize our children as arrows from Jesus, and God will be glorified. With these, usually fellow Christians, their hearts will be free to share the greatness of God.

A second group will not understand our children's character, and with these they should be careful. Some will be enemies of the gospel, hardened and warring against it, and our children should not "cast pearls before swine." Others will be ignorant, in need of the Word of God like a drought-stricken field needs rain. Jesus spoke to the crowds in parables, revealing their meaning to those who were thirsty, those who came to Him for a deeper understanding of the Water of Life. As our children learn to speak in ways that intrigue, they will put out a fishing line for the needy. If a person is curious and takes the bait, he may ask our children about their behavior. They should readily respond that Christ is their source of goodness, giving this soul what he needs to respond in faith.

The mark on the arrow is a deep etching, the character of Christ Himself, and those who don't know that strange mark may ask its meaning. Will your child be ready to give an answer?

I exercise my children in dialogue sessions, asking difficult questions and challenging their answers. We analyze sermons, political speeches, and newspaper articles, bantering about their points and logic. I allow the discussion to flow freely for a while, but I always steer it back toward my goal, preparing my children to defend the Word of God against the wisdom of the world. My hope is that they will be able to use their finely sharpened minds to answer any questions. When confession and character meet, they will prove the inborn mark of God, and the impact of the arrow will never be forgotten.

## ✦ Cleaving and Leaving

An arrow is fired. A child has left our shelter. Reasons for leaving can vary for each departing son or daughter, but one of the most common is to marry, to cleave to another man's child. As Jesus said, "For this cause a man shall leave his father and mother, and shall cleave to his wife; and the two shall become one flesh" (Matt. 19:5). God has so ordained the holy institution of marriage, and we would be well served to prepare for its wooing call to the altar.

Will our children eventually marry? The odds favor it. We who wish for grandchildren encourage it. God's implanted desire for a mate drives it. As our children mature, they will naturally begin to look favorably on members of the opposite sex, even desiring their company.

In our culture, boys and girls are usually left to themselves regarding romantic relationships. Dating is often allowed at ages so young the boy can barely see over the movie ticket window ledge to buy a pass for his diminutive date. Such unguided romance can lead to premarital sex, pregnancy, severe illness, painful breakups, or long-lasting emotional scars. What can we do to prevent this socially acceptable zeal for premarital coupling, this rush to hormonal fulfillment?

A father's role in helping a son or daughter find a life mate is a delicate responsibility, one that requires careful judgment. We want to prevent the damage the popular dating machine has wrought on our society, and we also want to create a positive impact, not just generate rules that say, "Thou shalt not!" Though a complete guide to that role is beyond the scope of this book, we can look at a few guidelines and brief reasons for each one.

1. Children should not have a romantic relationship until they are ready to be married. The reason for such a relationship is simple, to find a suitable mate. If a son or daughter is not ready to marry, then pursuing the opposite sex becomes recreational, a hunt for the good feelings that acceptance or fleshly indulgence can provide. Such recreation eventually leads to separation, pain, and broken faith. The youthful dating game rarely lasts longer than a season, and with each emotional bond that is shattered, a child is more fully trained to distrust the opposite sex, to dishonor the sanctity of emotional unity, and to disdain a romantic relationship as a long-lasting covenant. Simply put, dating is a training ground for divorce.

2. Thou shalt not date! Okay, I'm reverting to the law now with a rigid command that throws ten loops of chains around a teenager and claps on a Roman-numeral combination lock. The reasons for the command are few. The concept is simple. For what purpose should an unmarried boy and girl be alone? The only activities they can pursue that require privacy are activities we wish to prevent. It doesn't matter if they're getting together for milkshakes or to memorize Romans, being alone for the activity is unnecessary. It's the gateway to temptation, a snare in the weeds designed to pull

our children into the pit. There's no good reason to allow it. End of story.

3. A father inspects and decides whether or not to approve a suitor for his daughter, should both young man and young lady be of proper age and maturity. The gentleman must be serious about looking for a wife, not just hunting for personal pleasure and good times. If the father approves of the suitor, his daughter has the right to veto, asking her father to politely excuse the gentleman. The daughter is thereby protected from the pressure of rejecting an assertive pursuer. If the courtship arrangement is accepted, a father guides the couple's time together, assuring that the gentleman honors his commitment to pursue her heart with gentility of mind and purity of spirit.

4. A father counsels his son on the appropriate pursuit of a young lady, teaching him to follow courtship etiquette, to call on a young lady's father as the doorway to acceptance. If the lady's father is not willing to serve as a guide in the relationship, the son's father should step in and provide ongoing guidance for his son as he would for his daughter.

The list could go on. It could include how a father carefully watches over the heart of each child, for protection from those who would steal its affections, in prevention of the scars that unfulfilled promises leave in its vulnerable skin, and in preparation for sharing it with another in courtship and eventual union. If a father follows his own heart in watching over those of his children, making sure they understand the uniqueness and sanctity of cleaving flesh in marriage, honoring it even before the "I do's" are spoken, he will do well. The list of "Thou shalt not's!" will become a careful, guiding hand, not a fist of warning.

Fathers, fear not. The cleaving of marriage is a joy to anticipate! The marriage relationship is a holy union, one that reflects the bond between Christ and His church. Let us approach it with the loving energy of Christ's passion for His people. If we prepare our children to honor that union even as they seek its oneness, they will enter its loving embrace with hearts prepared to cleave in an inseparable melding of flesh, mind, and spirit.

## ✧ Busybody, Bailout, or Book?

The arrows have left your quiver; the fledglings have vacated your nest. You have given your counsel, and they have waved good-bye with thankful hearts. Some were brimming with confidence, excited about the future. Some left with tears, though with far fewer than you shed when you closed the door and faced your quiet home.

What do you do now? You've invested twenty, thirty, or forty years in your children, and now they're gone. Can you just let these treasures float away, dangling in dangers they've never faced alone?

As painful as it might be, yes. Put your pencils down, close your books, and turn in your papers. It's time for you to leave the class-room. Your grades will be posted in the halls of heaven.

It's a new life. The sorrow of vacancy blends with the joy of completion. How will you balance the two? So many parents live at one extreme or the other. Some are never able to let go, inter-fering in their adult children's business. They become busybodies, with noses protruding into their children's homes, jobs, and child rearing; they're cackling hens that never learned to stop scratch-ing for their chicks. Others simply abandon them, glad they're gone and out of their lives forever. These are bailouts, parents who feel as though they've been released from prison. Their liberty party lasts for years, and they're not available even if called upon for help.

A busybody father has no life of his own. He was wrapped up in his children, and their departure left him empty. He and his wife stare at each other, and they talk about the children, wondering why they don't call every day. They can't understand how their children can possibly live without them.

A bailout father probably never wanted his children in the first place. He was wrapped up in his own life, and their departure brought relief. Now that they're finally gone, he doesn't want anything to do with them. They'll do just fine.

When my children leave, I want to be a familiar old book. A book sits silently on the shelf and is available when needed. It's filled with stories and wise teaching. As a familiar book, its writings call out to be read when times are difficult. On a dark night, a child remembers its words and longs to hear them again.

The phone rings, and I hear, "Dad, the baby won't sleep! He cries all night. What do I do?"

With a silent laugh I reply, "You did the same thing. Strap him in the car seat and take him for a ride. That always worked for you."

The questions may be lighthearted, probing, or even painful. Yet, no matter how difficult the problem, if a child slides the book from the shelf, you have to be ready to help. Sometimes your help may come in the form of correction. In this new relationship, it should be a gentle prodding, since you're no longer the one in direct command. You're not in a position to enforce your will. But if his departure from God's path is manifested in obvious disobedience or apostasy, you may have to step in with a more forceful hand, becoming the voice of a prophet who warns of dire consequences. You were the voice of the judge in their lives before, and God may use you to remind a son or daughter of the deadly path of sin. At this point, if they're at the brink of apostasy, there's no need to worry about their reaction to your meddling. It's better to risk parental alienation than to risk their potential alienation from God.

You also have to be careful not to be a crutch. You shouldn't be trapped into daily baby-sitting or attached to the phone for hours with a crybaby son or daughter. Wisdom may tell you to say, "You already know the answer. You'll have to take care of this yourself." In this case, your help will be a push toward independence.

It will be gratifying to hear questions from your children, to glean news and learn how your arrows are flying, but your focus must turn elsewhere. You were a life-giver, a provider, a judge, a teacher, a savior. Those jobs are finished. Now you're a counselor. But you're not an activist counselor, in constant contact, trying to peddle your advice.

Can we be friends? I hope so. I'm nurturing friendship with my children, and I hope a close relationship will continue. This is the ideal—a loving, caring commitment between parents and children that abides even when we no longer share the same abode. Shall we paint this picture? Laughing together at picnics on grassy fields, teaching my grandchildren how to cast a fishing rod at a peaceful lake in the woods, sweating with my adult son as we dig an irrigation ditch together. God, help me do my part to keep our friendship growing.

But what if they disdain friendship? What do I do? I will not make myself a nuisance. I'll call from time to time, drop a note of encouragement, or maybe send a box of cookies. I'll remember birthdays and anniversaries with a card or a call, send invitations for special dinners on special days, or offer my help on a big project. I'll patiently allow days and weeks to go by without communication, because I'll realize they have lives of their own, and I have mine.

A life without the children? Yes, indeed. We were called to be stewards of our children, not owners. A steward's time eventually comes to a close, and he finds new employment. So it is for us. When the last child departs, a father joins with his wife to become full-time servants to church and community, creating a life that no longer revolves around a brood of little ones.

Yes, there will be sadness. When his feet step out my door, I'll remember when he tried on my shoes and clumped around the house, my shoe tops reaching above his ankles. When I hear his voice on the telephone asking for help, I'll remember his first cry in the hospital and my shouts of exhilaration. These memories will bring tears of joy, and more joy will follow. When I see a godly and compassionate man training his children the same way I trained him, I'll know that God has done a marvelous work, embedding His Word in my son's mind. When I see that legacy passed on to the next generation, then I'll know that the chain will go on. How great will be my joy! For through my humble stewardship, an army of gospel-bearing feet will follow the path of righteousness, the path that leads to the author and finisher of our faith, Jesus Christ.

## ✧ The Everlasting Song

It's spring again. That water oak still stands. The nest survives. Thick branches had enveloped the fragile network of twine and twigs, directing winter winds and drenching rains around its sheltering canopy. In curiosity I pull the branch, bending it down to eye level. I expect to see holes in the nest, the ravages of time and abandonment in a sad void that once held hope and happiness.

Three new eggs greet my eyes, and within seconds a frantic shriek zips past my ear. I gently release the branch and hurry away, looking back to see a pair of mockers scolding me with their emboldened fury. As one hops into the tree and out of sight, the other leaps to the summit with a flap of his wing. With a long note he begins his song, not the exact melody his father began when I first saw this nest, yet, it's the same story. Or is it a continuation of a story, a long journal begun by the first father bird at Eve's dawning?

When I finish my song, will my children carry it on? I have written the psalm with a pen of love, giving life, teaching, judging, saving, and guiding. Will their children share in the blessing from the lips of their fathers? Yes, if my own meager lips have spelled out the image of a father to my sons and to my daughters' husbands.

Sing it well, my children. It is not my song you sing; it is my Father's, my heavenly Father's own gracious hymn. He taught it to me. I sang it as I rocked your cradle, as I tied your shoes, as I wiped your tears, as I waved good-bye. My nest will never be empty while the words of that song fill the air, adding new stories to the legacy of God's everlasting love. Yes, my children, sing it well.

## ✧ Summary

Our children are like arrows, fired from a warrior's bow into the world. They need to be straight, instilled with the Word of God. Without accuracy, without guidance by a heavenly vision, they will miss the target. Only speed, being disciplined and self-motivated, will help them make an impact. Long-term goals will not be met without endurance, the ability to suffer through trials with the light of God within. And, finally, they will make eternal impressions because they'll be marked by God as being from Christ, carriers of the gospel.

When our children leave our fold, we become counselors, ready to share our wisdom as though we're books in a treasured library. We don't force them to take our advice like busybodies who have no other life, nor do we run away, bailing out of our responsibility to provide timely counsel. In a sense, we seek new employment, finding a ministry outside of parenting that will bring honor to God. As our children make their marks on the world, we rejoice that God has allowed us to prepare these arrows, to put them to string and propel them into the world. May God use them for His eternal glory as they pass on the legacy of His love.